The Charlton
Standard Catalogue of

ROYAL DOULTON BESWICK STORYBOOK FIGURINES

Third Edition

By
Jean Dale

Introduction
by
Louise Irvine

W. K. Cross
Publisher

The Charlton Press

Toronto, Ontario ✤ Birmingham, Michigan

Canadian Cataloguing In Publication Data

The Charlton price guide to Royal Doulton
and Beswick storybook figurines
Annual.
1994-
Issues for 1995-   have title: Charlton price guide
to Royal Doulton Beswick storybook figurines.
Cover title: Charlton standard catalogue of Royal
Doulton Beswick storybook figurines, 1995-   .
ISSN 1198-1652
ISBN 0-88968-163-5 (1996)

1. Porcelain animals - Catalogs. 2. Royal Doulton
figurines - Catalogs. I. Charlton Press. II. Title: Royal
Doulton Beswick storybook figurines. III. Title: Charlton
price guide to Royal Doulton Beswick storybook figurines.
IV. Title: Royal Doulton and Beswick storybook figures.
V. Title: Charlton standard catalogue of Royal Doulton
Beswick storybook figurines, 1995-   .

NK4660.C5   738.8'2'0294   C94-900402-2

EDITORIAL

Editor	Jean Dale
Editorial Assistant	Sandra Tooze
Graphic Technician	Patrick Glassford
Photography	Marilyn and Peter Sweet

ACKNOWLEDGEMENTS

The Charlton Press wishes to thank those who have helped with the third edition of *The Charlton Standard Catalogue of Royal Doulton Beswick Storybook Figurines.*

Special Thanks

The publisher would like to thank Louise Irvine for writing the introduction to this edition. Louise is an independent writer and lecturer on Royal Doulton's history and products and is not connected with the pricing in this price guide.

Our thanks also go to Royal Doulton (U.K.) Limited, which helped with additional technical information, especially Valerie Baynton, Katharine Ellis and Julie McKeown; Noel Tulner, Royal Doulton (U.S.A.) Limited; Pat O'Brien, Royal Doulton (Canada) Ltd. and Christine Tatton, Lawleys By Post.

Contributors to the Third Edition

The publisher would also like to thank the following individuals and companies who graciously supplied photographs or information or allowed us access to their collections for photographic purposes: George and Nora Bagnall, Precious Memories, Charlottetown, P.E.I.; Carolyn Baker, Richmond, VA; John and Diana Callow, England; Richard Dennis, Somerset, England; Mr. Gitterings, Cheshire, England; Ruth Huber, Portland Oregon; Mark Oliver, Phillips, London, England; Marilyn, Peter, Joanna and Natalie Sweet, Bolton, England; Leah Selig, Merrylands, Australia; Nick Tzimas, U. K. International Ceramics, Suffolk, England; Princess and Barry Weiss, New City, New York.

A SPECIAL NOTE TO COLLECTORS

We welcome and appreciate any comments or suggestions in regard to *The Charlton Standard Catalogue of Royal Doulton Beswick Storybook Figurines.* If any errors or omissions come to your attention, please write to us, or if you would like to participate in pricing or supply previously unavailable data or information, please contact Jean Dale at (416) 488-4653.

**Printed in Canada
in the Province of Quebec**

The Charlton Press

**Editorial Office
2010 Yonge Street
Toronto, Canada. M4S 1Z9
Telephone (416) 488-4653 Fax: (416) 488-4656
Telephone 800-442-6042 Fax: 800-442-1542**

HOW TO USE THIS PRICE GUIDE

THE PURPOSE

The third edition of this price guide covers the complete range of children's figures issued by Royal Doulton and Beswick. In the process we have taken liberties with the name of this catalogue, for all figures listed are certainly not derived from storybook characters. However, the great majority are, and thus we have carried the name forward.

As with the other catalogues in Charlton's Royal Doulton reference and pricing library, this publication has been designed to serve two specific purposes. First, to furnish the collector with accurate and detailed listings that provide the essential information needed to build a rewarding collection. Second, to provide collectors and dealers with current market prices for the complete line of Doulton and Beswick storybook figures.

STYLES AND VERSIONS

STYLES: A change in style occurs when a major element of the design is altered or modified as a result of a deliberate mould change. An example of this is *The Duchess With Flowers* (style one) and *The Duchess With a Pie* (style two).

VERSIONS: Versions are modifications in a minor style element, such as the long ears becoming short ears on *Mr. Benjamin Bunny*.

VARIATIONS: A change in colour is a variation; for example, *Mr. Jeremy Fisher's* change in colourways from spotted to striped leggings.

THE LISTINGS

The Beatrix Potter figures are arranged alphabetically. At the beginning of the Beatrix Potter listings are two pages graphically outlining backstamp variations. Backstamps are illustrated for seven different varieties covering over fifty years of production. In the Beatrix Potter pricing charts, the reader will see Beswick and Doulton model numbers, backstamp numbers and market prices.

The Brambly Hedge figures are listed by their DBH numbers. There are no backstamp variations known.

The Bunnykins figures are arranged in numerical order by DB numbers, with the exception of the first six, which were issued in the late 1930s. These are *Billy, Farmer, Freddie, Mary, Mother* and *Reggie*, and they are arranged alphabetically. There are six different backstamps used on the Bunnykins figures. Please see the section on backstamp variations at the beginning of the Bunnykins listings.

The Snowman series is listed in numerical order by the DS numbers. There are no backstamp variations.

All of the above listings include the modeller, where known, the name of the animal figure, designer, height, colour, date of issue, varieties and series.

A WORD ON PRICING

The purpose of this catalogue is to give readers the most accurate, up-to-date retail prices for storybook figures in the United States, Canada, the United Kingdom and Australia.

To accomplish this, The Charlton Press continues to access an international pricing panel of experts who submit prices based on both dealer and collector retail-price activity, as well as current auction results in the U. S., Canada, the U. K. and Australia for the Bunnykins markets. These market prices are carefully averaged to reflect accurate valuations for figures in each of these markets. All discontinued figures are priced in this manner.

Current figures are priced according to the manufacturer's suggested retail price in each of the four market regions. Please be aware that price or promotional sales discounting is always possible and can result in lower prices than those listed.

The prices published herein are for figures in mint condition. Collectors are cautioned that a repaired or restored piece may be worth as little as 50 percent of the value of the same figure in mint condition.

A further word on pricing. As mentioned previously, this is a catalogue giving prices for figures in the currency of a particular market (U.S. dollars for the American market and sterling for the U.K. market). The bulk of the prices given herein are not determined by currency exchange calculations, but by actual market activity in the market concerned.

One exception, however, occurs in the case of current figures or recent limited editions issued in only one of the four markets. Since such items were priced by Doulton only in the country in which they were to be sold, prices for the other markets are not shown.

Additionally, collectors must remember that all relevant information must be known to make a proper valuation of price. When comparing auction prices to catalogue prices, collectors and dealers must remember two important points. First, compare "apples and apples." Be sure that auction prices realized for figures include a buyer's premium if one is due. Buyer's premiums can range from 10 to 15 percent, and on an expensive piece this amount can be substantial. Secondly, know whether a figure is restored, repaired or in mint condition. This fact may not be noted or explained in the listings, and as a result, its price will not be reflective of that same piece in mint condition. Please be aware of repairs and restorations and the effect they may have on values.

A last word of caution. No pricing catalogue can be, or should be, a fixed price list. This catalogue must be considered a pricing guide only—showing the most current retail prices based on market demand within a particular region for the various figures.

CONTENTS

INTRODUCTION
By Louise Irvine

THE HISTORY OF STORYBOOK CHARACTERS FROM THE ROYAL DOULTON, JOHN BESWICK AND ROYAL ALBERT STUDIOS

For over a century, the Royal Doulton Studios have entertained us with storybook characters, particularly animals endowed with human personalities. In Victorian times, a group of frogs enacting a well-known fable raised a smile in much the same way as the antics of the BRAMBLY HEDGE™ mice amuse us today. The tales of BEATRIX POTTER™, with lots of different animals acting and conversing as if they were human, are as popular now as when they were first written in the early 1900s. Similarly the BUNNYKINS™ characters, first created in the 1930s, have survived the vagaries of fashion to become the most popular collectables of the 1990s. Obviously the idea of a creature simultaneously human and animal is deep rooted in our literary culture, and it is interesting to trace when it first became apparent in the Doulton world.

A Tinmouth mouse group

The Doulton factory was founded in London in 1815, but for the first 50 years production was confined to practical pottery. In the late 1860s, Sir Henry Doulton established an art studio, employing students from the Lambeth School of Art to decorate vases, jugs and plaques in fashionable Victorian styles. Some artists specialised in figurative sculpture, notably George Tinworth, who was the first to seek inspiration from

well-known stories. The Bible provided him with most of his subject matter, but he also enjoyed reading the fables of Aesop and La Fontaine. These moralistic tales feature foxes, mice, lions and other creatures exemplifying human traits, and they fascinated the Victorians, particularly after the publication of Darwin's theory of evolution. Tinworth modelled several fables groups in the 1880s, including *The Fox and the Ape*, *The Cat and the Cheese* and *The Ox and the Frogs*. Later he produced mice and frog subjects, based on his own observations of human nature, which reflect his perceptive sense of humour.

The potential for dressed-up animals to disguise a deeper message soon led to their widespread use in children's literature, notably *Alice's Adventures in Wonderland* and Lear's nonsense poems. In 1908, Kenneth Grahame wrote *Wind in the Willows* to comment on the behaviour of the English aristocracy, but the exciting adventures of Mr. Toad subtly conceal the author's critical stance. The dapper toad in his pinstripes and tails was modelled shortly afterwards by Lambeth artist Francis Pope, and a companion piece shows Mr. Toad disguised as a washerwoman in order to escape from prison.

Mr. Toad disguised as a washerwoman

Figures like these probably encouraged Beatrix Potter to approach the Lambeth studio in 1908 with a view to having her own animal characters immortalised in ceramic. Miss Potter published several illustrated stories about her favourite animals after the success of *The Tale* of *Peter Rabbit*™ in 1902, and some characters had already appeared as cuddly toys and decorative motifs on clothes, etc. Unfortunately an earlier contract with a German china firm made any arrangement with Doulton impossible, but she tried on a later occasion to have figures made of her characters at Grimwade's factory in Stoke-on-Trent. They suggested that Doulton's other factory in Burslem would be the best place to have the figures decorated, but again plans fell through. It was not until after Miss Potter's death that her dream was realised when the John Beswick factory in Longton began making little figures inspired by her books.

The John Beswick factory was founded in 1894 to produce ornamental jugs, vases and other decorative fancies. By the 1940s the Beswick artists had established a reputation for quality animal modelling, particularly portraits of famous horses by Arthur Gredington. In 1947, Gredington demonstrated his versatility when he modelled *Jemima Puddleduck* at the suggestion of Lucy Beswick, the wife of the managing director. She had been inspired by a visit to Beatrix Potter's Lake District home, where many of the tales are set. The success of this first study led to an initial collection of ten Beatrix Potter characters, including *Peter Rabbit, Benjamin Bunny* and *Mrs. Tiggy Winkle.*

A group of Beatrix Potter books with the figures beside

Launched in 1948, the new Beatrix Potter figures were welcomed with enthusiasm, and it was not long before Gredington was at work on another collection of character animals, this time from an American animated film. The *Lion* cartoon by David Hand was released in 1948, and Zimmy the Lion became a new star for the Rank Film Organisation. Sequel cartoons introduced Ginger Nutt, Hazel Nutt, Dinkum Platypus, Loopy Hare, Oscar Ostrich, Dusty Mole and Felia Cat, all of which were modelled in 1949 as the *DAVID HAND'S ANIMALAND*™ series. David Hand had formerly worked for the Walt Disney studios, directing Mickey Mouse shorts, as well as the major films *Snow White* and

Bambi, and it was not long before these cartoons also inspired a collection of Beswick figures. Arthur Gredington modelled the little figures of *Snow White and the Seven Dwarfs* whilst Jan Granoska, a trainee modeller, was given the task of portraying Mickey Mouse and friends, plus some characters from *Pinocchio* and *Peter Pan.* Although Miss Granoska was only at the Beswick studio for three years, she was responsible for some of their most desirable figures.

Music (of sorts!) is being played by the BEDTIME CHORUS™, a group of enthusiastic children accompanied by a singing cat and dog. These were amongst the first character figures to be modelled by Albert Hallam, who gradually took over responsibility for this area in the 1960s. As head mouldmaker, Hallam had made many of the production moulds for Gredington designs, so he was already familiar with the subject matter. He continued the *Beatrix Potter* collection, adding characters such as *Old Mr. Brown* and *Cecily Parsley,* and in 1968 he launched a new Disney series based on their newest cartoon hit, *Winnie the Pooh and the Blustery Day.*

The late 1960s was a time of transition for the company, as Ewart Beswick was ready to retire but he had no heir for his successful business. Fortunately the Royal Doulton group was in the midst of an expansion programme and they acquired the Beswick factory in 1969. They soon benefited from Beswick's expertise in the field of character animals, as Albert Hallam began modelling little figures inspired by their famous Bunnykins nurseryware.

The Bunnykins characters were originally created in the 1930s by Barbara Vernon, a young nun who taught in an English convent school. She often entertained her pupils with sketches and stories about the Bunnykins characters and their potential as nurseryware decoration was recognised by her father Cuthbert Bailey, who was Doulton's managing director at the time. Bunnykins was launched in 1934 and, sixty years later, it is still one of the world's best-selling nurseryware patterns.

Artist Bunnykins with the nurseyware plate

There had been an attempt in 1939 to start a collection of Bunnykins figures, but the Second World War intervened and production was not resumed, making the first six characters very rare indeed. Nine new style figures by Albert Hallam were launched in 1972, followed by three more the following year, and they were all derived from characters in the Bunnykins nurseryware scenes. When Albert Hallam retired in 1975, Graham Tongue became the head modeller at the Beswick Studio under Harry Sales, newly appointed as design manager.

Harry Sales was primarily a graphic artist and he dreamed up many new ideas for Bunnykins figures, which Graham Tongue and others modelled during the 1980s. He created a new adult audience for Bunnykins with his witty sporting subjects, for example *Jogging Bunnykins* and *Bogey Bunnykins,* and as collector interest grew, he began to design special commissions, such as *Uncle Sam* and *Collector Bunnykins.* At the same time, he was responsible for the continued development of the Beatrix Potter range, which was becoming increasingly difficult as the most popular characters had already been modelled. Favourites, such as *Peter Rabbit* and *Jemima Puddleduck,* were introduced in new poses, and he came up with the idea of double figures, for example *Mr Benjamin Bunny and Peter Rabbit* and *Tabitha Twitchet and Miss Moppet.*

As well as developing the established figure collections, Harry Sales delved into lots of other children's books for inspiration. He reinterpreted the timeless characters from classic tales such as *Alice's Adventures in Wonderland* and *Wind in the Willows,* and he worked from contemporary picture books, notably Joan Walsh Anglund's *A Friend is Someone Who Likes You* and Norman Thelwell's *Angels on Horseback.* Whenever possible, Harry liaised closely with the originators of the characters he portrayed. He spent many happy hours of research at Thelwell's studio, studying his cartoons of shaggy ponies with comical riders, and he also worked with Alfred Bestall, the illustrator of the Rupert Bear adventures in the *Daily Express* newspaper before embarking on this series in 1980.

With their outstanding reputation for developing character animals, it is not surprising that Royal Doulton artists were invited to work on the publishing sensation of the 1980s, the Brambly Hedge stories by Jill Barklem. Within three years of their launch the spring, summer, autumn and winter stories had been reprinted 11 times, translated into ten languages, and had sold in excess of a million copies. Readers young and old were captivated by the enchanting world of the Brambly Hedge mice, as indeed was Harry Sales, whose job it was to recreate the characters in the ceramic medium. In his own words, "The first time I read the books and studied the illustrations I felt that I was experiencing something quite unique. Over a period of many years designing for the pottery industry one develops an awareness, a 'feeling' for that something special. Brambly Hedge had this."

Ideas flowed quickly and eight leading characters were chosen from the seasonal stories for the initial collection, which was launched in 1983. Such was the response that they were soon joined by six more subjects, making a total of 14 by 1986, when Harry left the company. Graham Tongue succeeded him as design manager and has continued to add new Brambly Hedge figures from the original stories on a regular basis. Miss Barklem's later titles, *The Secret Staircase, The High Hills* and *The Sea Story,* have also provided inspiration for some of the more recent figures; for example, *Mr and Mrs Saltapple* supply the Brambly Hedge community with salt in *The Sea Story.*

Encouraged by the amazing success of the Brambly Hedge collection, Royal Doulton's marketing executives were soon considering other new storybook characters. Like millions of TV viewers, they were spellbound by the magical film, *The Snowman,* which was first screened in 1982. Based on the illustrated book of the same name by Raymond Briggs, the animated film about a snowman who comes to life has become traditional Christmas entertainment in many parts of the world. The absence of words gives the tale a haunting quality, and there is hardly a dry eye in the house when the little boy, James, awakes to find his Snowman friend has melted away after an exciting night exploring each other's worlds. Fortunately the SNOWMAN™ lives on in more durable form in the Royal Doulton collection. Again Harry Sales was given the challenge of transforming this amorphous character into ceramic, whilst remaining faithful to Briggs' original soft crayon drawings. He succeeded in this difficult task by adding additional curves to the contours of the figures which gives them a life-like appearance. The first four figures were ready and approved by Raymond Briggs in 1985, and the collection grew steadily until 1990, latterly under the direction of Graham Tongue.

So far the 1990s has seen Graham Tongue and his team of artists developing the Beatrix Potter and Bunnykins collections for two major anniversaries—the 100th birthday of *Peter Rabbit* and the diamond jubilee of Bunnykins in 1994. Also in 1994, the centenary of the Beswick factory was marked with the launch of the *Pig Promenade,* featuring a special commemorative backstamp.

This series is just one of three new collections of novelty figures, and it is refreshing to see this traditional type of Beswick ware being revitalised by a new generation of artists. Amanda Hughes-Lubeck and Warren Platt created the LITTLE LOVABLES™, a series of cute clowns with special messages, such as "Good Luck" and "Congratulations," and they also worked with Martyn Alcock on the collection of ENGLISH COUNTRY FOLK™, which has been very well received.

The collecting of Beatrix Potter and Bunnykins figures has reached epidemic proportions in recent years, and there is now a growing awareness of the desirability of all their storybook cousins, hence the need for this much expanded price guide.

COLLECTING BEATRIX POTTER FIGURES

A number of factors have combined recently to make Beatrix Potter figures the "hottest" collectables of the 1990s. The 100th birthday of *Peter Rabbit* was celebrated amidst a storm of publicity in 1993, and the first reference book on the Beswick and Royal Albert figures was launched to coincide with all the celebrations. In addition, the centenary of the John Beswick factory in 1994 focused a lot of collector attention on its products.

The market has been stimulated by recent withdrawals from the range—12 were announced at the end of 1993, and six at the end of 1994, making a total of 30 retired figures to date. Prices are rocketing for the early discontinued figures, and most collectors will need a bank loan to purchase *Duchess with Flowers*, the first Beatrix Potter figure to be retired, if indeed they are lucky enough to find one for sale.

Ever since the Beswick factory launched their Beatrix Potter collection in 1948, most of the figures have been bought as gifts for children. However, many young fans have grown up to find they have some very valuable figures, with early modelling and backstamp variations, and they have begun collecting in earnest to fill the gaps and find the rarities. Figures marked with a Beswick backstamp are most in demand, as this trademark was replaced with the Royal Albert backstamp in 1989. The Royal Albert factory, another famous name in the Doulton group, produces all the Beatrix Potter tableware, and the change of backstamps was made for distribution reasons. The most desirable Beswick marks are the gold varieties, which predate 1972, and these are often found on early modelling or colour variations, which also attract a premium price, for example, *Mrs Rabbit* with her umbrella sticking out and *Mr Benjamin Bunny* with his pipe protruding.

As well as seeking out discontinued figures and rare variations, it is advisable to keep up to date with new models as they are introduced. A complete Beatrix Potter figure collection will encompass 96 of the standard-size models, around three inches tall, and eight large models, which are about twice the size. *Peter Rabbit*, the first of these large size models, was launched in 1993 with a special commemorative backstamp from the John Beswick studio, and it changed in 1994 to the standard Royal Albert mark.

If owning all the Beatrix Potter figures is beyond the realms of possibility, whether for financial or display limitations, then why not focus on particular types of animals or characters from your favourite tales. There are twenty mice figures to find, a dozen cat characters and more than twenty rabbits, including seven portraits of *Peter Rabbit* to date. There are also discontinued character jugs, relief modelled plaques and a ceramic display stand to look out for, so happy hunting.

COLLECTING BUNNYKINS FIGURES

The diamond jubilee of Bunnykins brought the famous rabbit family into the limelight once again, and a special *60th Anniversary Bunnykins*, proudly carrying a birthday cake, was just one of eight new figures released in 1994. Even more are planned for 1997, and this wide variety of introductions is indicative of today's tremendous enthusiasm for collecting Bunnykins. When the DB range was launched in 1972, most of the figures were purchased to amuse young children, but the sporting characters of the 1980s began to appeal to adults and, in many cases, exchanging whimsical gifts developed into serious collecting.

Harry Sales drawing for Collector Bunnykins

The golden jubilee celebrations in 1984 introduced Bunnykins to an even wider audience, and led to the first collectors book, published by Richard Dennis. Fans were introduced to the entire range of nurseryware and figures, including the six large-size models from 1939, which are extremely hard to find. Apart from these elusive models, it was relatively easy to form a complete collection of figures in the mid 1980s, as the DB range consisted of just 28 models with only four withdrawals. *Autumn Days, Springtime, The Artist* and *Grandpa's Story*, withdrawn in 1982 and 1983, are now very sought after on the secondary market, but subsequent developments have generated much rarer characters. In 1986, Royal Doulton USA ordered new colourways of *Mr and Mrs Easter Bunnykins* to sell at a programme of artist demonstrations, and these are now extremely difficult to find. Similarly, the two special colourways of *Bedtime Bunnykins*, made for D. H. Holmes and Belks department stores in 1987 and 1988, are now increasing in price as serious collectors try to get hold of them.

Although most Bunnykins characters are modelled with young children in mind, there have been several subjects exclusively for collectors, notably *Collector Bunnykins* which was commissioned by the International Collectors Club in 1987. As it was only offered for a six month period, it is now one of the rarest models in the DB range. *The Royal Doulton Collectors Band*, featuring the first limited-edition Bunnykins figures, was launched at the London Doulton Fair in 1990, and since then there have been several limited pieces for exclusive distribution and special occasions. The overwhelming response to these special commissions was highlighted last year when the *Sergeant Mountie Bunnykins* sold out within hours of its launch at the Canadian Doulton show. Similarly, many of the limited editions commissioned by UK International Ceramics are now fully subscribed.

With this in mind, it is a good idea to buy the new Bunnykins figures as soon as they are issued. Royal Doulton has now allocated more than 150 DB numbers and, although a few intervening numbers have not been issued, notably *Ballet Bunnykins*, DB 44, committed collectors now have quite a challenge to find them all. Figures are now regularly withdrawn from the range, adding to the excitement of the chase and, like many fellow collectors, you can always dream of finding all the rare 1939 models!

COLLECTING BRAMBLY HEDGE FIGURES

Since their introduction in 1983, the Brambly Hedge mice have overrun households in many parts of the world. They are scurrying about the shelves as Royal Doulton figures and even climbing up the walls on decorative plates. Far from being undesirable, these particular mice are considered indispensable members of the family. Children frequently receive them as gifts from doting grandparents, but adults have also been seduced by the cosy, timeless mouse world which Jill Barklem has created. The mood of rustic nostalgia has all been painstakingly researched. The interiors of the field mice homes are of the sort common in English farmhouses at the end of the 19th century, and the food served is genuine country fare, based on old recipes and tasted in Jill Barklem's kitchen. The Brambly Hedge residents were all expertly drawn with the aid of her two mouse models, a keen understanding of zoology and a knowledge of historical costume.

The same attention to detail went into the Royal Doulton figures designed by Harry Sales. As he explains, "One important feature in the concept was that I chose poses which, when the figures are together, appear to be reacting to one another. I can imagine the fun children and the young at heart will have arranging the figures in conversational situations." Essentially this sums up the collectability of the Brambly Hedge mice, and the size of the series means they can all still be displayed effectively together on one shelf. To date there have been 25 little figures, and all are still relatively affordable, although the eight withdrawals are beginning to have an impact on the secondary market. There is one unusual modelling variation to look out for, as *Mr Toadflax's* tail was altered shortly after its introduction.

COLLECTING SNOWMAN FIGURES

The seasonal appeal of the Snowman has tended to limit his collectability, as most purchases are made around Christmas time, and he is more popular in areas which regularly experience snow. Having said this, for some fans the wintry connotations are overshadowed by the inherent quality and humour of the models and there are keen collectors in sunny Florida as well as in Australia, where beach barbecues are typical Christmas celebrations.

Between 1985 and 1990, young children regularly received the new Snowman models in their Christmas stockings, and the characters have been widely used as holiday decorations. Like the Brambly Hedge models, they were designed to interact, and the little figure of *James*, gazing up in wonder can be positioned with various Snowman characters, whilst the band works very well as a separate display grouping. There are 19 figures and two musical boxes to collect and, as the range has now all been withdrawn, they can now be quite difficult to locate. After a gap of four years, a new type of Snowman collectable was launched in July 1994, in the form of a miniature character jug by Martyn Alcock. Perhaps this will be the catalyst to a renewed interest in the Snowman collection.

COLLECTING STORYBOOK CHARACTERS

The Beatrix Potter, Brambly Hedge and Snowman stories have already been discussed in some detail, as there are so many figures to collect in each of the categories. However, the Beswick artists have also sought inspiration in other children's stories, some better known than others.

The American author-illustrator, Joan Walsh Anglund, enjoyed quite a vogue in the 1960s following the publication of *A Friend is Someone Who Likes You* (1958). Three of her drawings of cute children with minimal features were modelled by Albert Hallam for the Beswick range in 1969, but they were withdrawn soon after, making them extremely hard to find today.

The bizarre cast of characters from *Alice's Adventures in Wonderland* has offered a lot more scope for collectors. First published in 1865, this classic tale has entertained generations of young readers and inspired many artistic interpretations. In the early 1900s, Doulton's Lambeth artists modelled some fantastic creatures from the tale, notably the pig-like *Rath* from the "Jabberwocky" poem. The Burslem studio designed an extensive series of nurseryware and, more recently, a collection of character jugs based on the original illustrations by Sir John Tenniel, who firmly fixed the appearance of the Wonderland characters in the public imagination. Harry Sales also consulted the Tenniel illustrations in 1973 when designing Beswick's ALICE IN WONDERLAND™ series. The resulting 11 figures faithfully capture the spirit of the book and remained a popular set in the range until 1983.

Curiously the figures inspired by another great children's classic, *Wind in the Willows*, did not have the same appeal. Christina Thwaites, a young book illustrator, was commissioned to produce designs for a collection of wall plates and tea wares, and her watercolours of Mr Toad, Ratty, Mole, Badger and others were interpreted by the Beswick modellers. Four figures were launched in 1987 and two more in 1988 as part of a co-ordinated giftware range with the Royal Albert backstamp, but they were withdrawn in 1989.

Consequently *Portly* and *Weasel*, the later introductions, were only made for one year, and will no doubt prove particularly hard to find in the future.

With the WIND IN THE WILLOWS™ collection, the Royal Doulton artists have come full circle, reflecting the enthusiasm of their predecessors at Lambeth, notably Francis Pope who modelled two superb figures of Mr Toad shortly after the book was published. Obviously storybook characters, particularly animals in human guises, have timeless appeal.

COLLECTING CARTOON CHARACTERS

Cartoon characters, whether they be from animated films or comic book strips, are becoming a popular field for collectors. The forthcoming book on the subject, together with introductions, such as *Tom and Jerry*, will surely generate even more interest. Now is the time to start collecting, if you have not already done so.

The characters from David Hand's Animaland are virtually unknown today, but following their film debut in 1948, they were sufficiently well known to inspire Beswick's first series of cartoon figures. Modelled in 1949 and withdrawn in 1955, *Zimmy the Lion* and his seven friends now have a different kind of notoriety, stealing the show when they come up for auction.

In contrast, Mickey Mouse is the best known cartoon character in the world. Within a year of his 1928 screen debut in *Steamboat Willie*, his image was being used to endorse children's products, and by the 1950s there were more than 3,000 different Mickey Mouse items, including plates, dolls, watches and clothes. With all this merchandising activity, it is not surprising that the Beswick studio sought a license for portraying Mickey and his friends in ceramic.

A range of nurseyware was launched in 1954, along with figures of *Mickey* and his girlfriend *Minnie*, *Pluto* his dog and his crazy friends *Goofy* and *Donald Duck*. Characters from some of Walt Disney's feature-length cartoons completed the original WALT DISNEY CHARACTERS™ set of 12 figures. *Peter Pan*, the newest Disney hit in 1953, inspired four characters, *Peter* himself, *Tinkerbell*, *Smee* and *Nana*, whilst the classic *Pinocchio* (1940) provided the puppet hero and his insect conscience *Jiminy Cricket*. Surprisingly only *Thumper* was modelled from another favourite film, *Bambi* (1942), although the fawn appears on the tableware designs. The response to the initial Disney collection encouraged the Beswick factory to launch a second set the following year, featuring *Snow White and the Seven Dwarfs* from Disney's first feature symphony. All the Disney characterisations are superb, making them extremely desirable amongst collectors of Beswick and Disneyana and they are all hard to find, even though they were produced until 1967.

The 1960s saw the rise of a new Disney star, Winnie the Pooh, who became a very popular merchandising character after his cartoon debut in 1966. The Beswick factory was quick off the mark, launching an initial collection of six characters from the film in 1968, followed by two more in 1971. "The Bear of Little Brain" originated in bedtime stories about nursery toys told by AA Milne to his son Christopher Robin in the 1920s, and he was visualised in the resulting books by the illustrator E.H. Shepard. Royal Doulton recently launched a range of nurseryware with scenes adapted from the *Winnie the Pooh* books and more developments are planned in the future.

The massive marketing campaigns for Disney characters have made them household names all over the world. British cartoon characters, by comparison, are less well known internationally. The *Daily Express* newspaper was slow to capitalise on the success of Rupert the Bear, who has been the star of their children's comic strip since 1920. Originated by Mary Tourtel, the Rupert stories were enlivened by Alfred Bestall who took over the daily drawings in 1935. Rupert enjoys the most extraordinary adventures with his friends Bill the Badger, Algy Pug and Pong-Ping, always returning safely to his comfortable family home in Nutwood. Rupert Bear annuals sold in millions from the mid 1930s, and his exploits were adapted for TV in the 1970s, but his following is essentially British. No doubt it was for this reason that the five figures in the RUPERT THE BEAR™ collection, designed by Harry Sales in 1980, were relatively short lived.

A similar fate befell the NORMAN THELWELL™ figures, which were in production from 1981 to 1989. Norman Thelwell was a humorous illustrator for *Punch* magazine, who made his reputation with comical observations of young riders and their mounts. *Angels on Horseback*, published in 1957, was the first compilation of his successful cartoons, and many other popular books followed. Thelwell worked closely with Harry Sales to create the most effective figures, both in ceramic and resin, and the results are guaranteed to raise a smile without breaking the bank.

After a gap of nearly 15 years, famous cartoon characters are back on the drawing board at the Royal Doulton studios once again. *Denis the Menace* and *Desperate Dan*, stars of the long-established children's comics, *The Beano* and *The Dandy*, have been immortalised as character jugs. This is the first time large-size character jugs have been used for portraying cartoons, although there are similarities to the set of six THUNDERBIRDS™ busts modelled by jug designer Bill Harper to celebrate the 30th anniversary of this children's TV show in 1992.

COLLECTING CHARACTER ANIMALS

In the 1880s Doulton's first artist, George Tinworth, was modelling groups of mice engaged in popular human pastimes, and nearly a century later Kitty MacBride did much the same thing with her *Happy Mice*. The appeal of these anthropomorphic creatures is timeless, and collectors have responded with enthusiasm from Victorian times to the present day. Admittedly, developing a taste for Tinworth's sense of humour will prove very expensive, with models costing several hundreds of pounds each, but the KITTY MACBRIDE™ whimsical mice are still relatively affordable.

Kitty MacBride was a writer and illustrator who began to model little clay figures of mice in 1960. Initially they were sold through a London dealer, but when she could not keep up with the demand she asked the Beswick factory to produce 11 of them commercially, which they did between 1975 and 1983.

The Beswick studio has had a considerable reputation for character animals since the launch of the Beatrix Potter collection in 1948. However, the modellers have not only interpreted illustrations from famous books, from time to time they have envisaged their own comical creatures. Albert Hallam was responsible for a succession of animals with human expressions in the late 1960s. Similar humanising traits can be found in the LITTLE LIKABLES™ collection, which was produced briefly in the mid 1980s. Robert Tabbenor's animals play up the humour of their situation, notably the carefree frog, *Watching the World Go By*, whilst Diane Griffiths takes a more sentimental approach, using human feelings to describe her cartoon-like animals.

The fun has continued in recent years with a collection of footballer cats, produced in 1987 only, and the on-going series of English Country Folk, depicting appropriate animals with human manners and costumes. However, the last laugh is reserved for the Pig Promenade. The absurdity of nine 'different breeds of pigs playing musical instruments makes this one of the most hilarious series of character animals.

MAKING STORYBOOK CHARACTERS

All the current storybook characters are made at the John Beswick factory in Longton, which became part of the Royal Doulton group in 1969. They have over fifty years' experience in the production of humorous figures and character animals, and essentially the methods have not changed since the earliest days of the Beatrix Potter figures.

First of all the designer has to familiarise himself thoroughly with the character to be portrayed, reading the story and studying the illustration. Having chosen the most suitable pose for interpretation in ceramic, he will produce reference drawings for the modeller. Often he can only see one side of the character in the original illustration, so he has to improvise for his three-dimensional model.

In consultation with the designer, the modeller will create the figure in modelling clay, and if satisfactory, a set of master moulds will be made in plaster of Paris. The number of mould parts will depend on the complexity of the figure, and sometimes the head and arms have to be moulded separately. Two or three prototype figures will be cast from the master mould for colour trials and subsequent approval by the original artist or his agent.

In the case of the Beatrix Potter figures, all the models are scrutinised by the licensing agents, Copyrights, working on behalf of Miss Potter's original publishers, Frederick Warne. Raymond Briggs, who was responsible for the Snowman, is generally quite relaxed about letting experts in other media interpret his drawings. He thought Royal Doulton's models were marvellous and really captured the spirit of the story, although he maintained he would "jolly well say so" if he thought they had got it wrong! Jill Barklem, the creator of Brambly Hedge, likes to get very involved in the licensing of her characters, and design manager Harry Sales spent a lot of time working with her on the finer points of detail. Sometimes slight modifications need to be made to the model or the colour scheme before the figure is approved by all concerned.

The next stage is to produce plaster of Paris working moulds from the master, and supplies are sent to the casting department. An earthenware body is used to cast all the character figures produced at the John Beswick studio, and it is poured into the mould in liquid form, known as slip. The moisture in the slip is absorbed into the plaster of Paris moulds and a "skin" of clay forms the interior.

Once the clay has set to the required thickness, the excess clay is poured out and the mould is carefully dismantled. Any separate mould parts, such as projecting arms, will be joined on at this stage using slip as an adhesive, and the seams will be gently sponged away. The figure is then allowed to dry slowly before it goes for its first firing. The high temperature in the kiln drives out the moisture in the body and the figure shrinks by about 1/12th of its original size, forming a hard "biscuit" body.

Skilled decorators will paint the figure, using special under-glaze ceramic colours. They work from an approved colour sample and great care is taken to match the colours to the original book illustrations. A second firing hardens on the colour before the figure is coated with a solution of liquid glaze. When the figure is fired in the glost kiln, it emerges with a shiny transparent finish which enhances and permanently protects the vibrant colours underneath. After a final inspection, the figures are dispatched to china shops all over the world where they will capture the hearts of collectors young and old.

RESIN FIGURES

Several collectables manufacturers began experimenting with new sculptural materials in the 1980s and developed different types of resin bodies that allow more intricately modelled detail than conventional ceramic processes. Royal Doulton launched its new "bonded ceramic body" in 1984, and two storybook collections were included in its Beswick Studio Sculptures, as the range was known. Seven subjects were chosen from the *Tales of Beatrix Potter* and two from the Thelwell series, but production was short lived, despite the minute detailing of the animals' fur and the tiny pebbles and grasses in their habitat, which would have been impossible to achieve in traditional earthenware. Royal Doulton ceased production of resin at the end of 1985, but it did commission 12 little Beswick Bears, which were only available in 1993.

BUYING CURRENT AND DISCONTINUED STORYBOOK CHARACTERS

The Royal Doulton Company owns many well-known china factories, including John Beswick, Royal Albert and Royal Doulton itself, and different trademarks are used for historical reasons or depending on the type of product. The Bunnykins, Brambly Hedge and Snowman collections feature the Royal Doulton backstamp, the Pig Promenade and English Country Folk carry a Beswick backstamp, whilst the Beatrix Potter figures, originally part of the Beswick range, are now marked Royal Albert. All these varied collections are produced at the John Beswick factory in Longton, Stoke-on-Trent, and models still being made at the factory today are referred to as "current." Most of the current storybook figures can be purchased in specialist china shops or from mail-order companies specialising in collectables. However, some Bunnykins figures have been commissioned for exclusive distribution, notably the special editions for UK International Ceramics, and these are available direct from this company in the UK or from its appointed agents overseas.

Up-to-date information about new introductions to the storybook collections is included in *Gallery* magazine, which is published quarterly by the Royal Doulton International Collectors Club. The Club regularly commissions exclusive collectables for its membership, and Bunnykins figures have been featured in the past. Members also receive information about withdrawals to the collection in the various branch newsletters.

Once a piece has been withdrawn from production, it is referred to as "discontinued" or "retired," and it enters the secondary market. Many specialist Royal Doulton dealers around the world carry discontinued storybook characters. Some have shops or showrooms, but most sell by mail order and exhibit regularly at antique shows. Some of the more expensive Bunnykins and Beatrix Potter figures are now being sold at auction, notably *Duchess with Flowers*. Most storybook characters do not yet qualify for the minimum lot price but it is still worth watching out for group lots at auctions or estate sales, in case some of the character animals have been included. Perhaps a rare Beatrix Potter or Bunnykins colourway will not be recognised as such!

WHERE TO BUY

Discontinued storybook figures can be found in antique shops, markets and fairs, as well as at auction houses. Specialist dealers in these figures attend many of the venues and events below.

UNITED KINGDOM
Auction Houses

Phillips
101 New Bond Street
London W1

Christie's South Kensington
85 Old Brompton Road
London SW5

Bonhams
Montpelier Street
London SW7

Sotheby's
Summer's Place
Billingshurst, West Sussex

Louis Taylor
Percy Street
Hanley, Stoke-on-Trent

Peter Wilson
Victoria Gallery
Market Street
Nantwich, Cheshire

Antique Fairs

U.K. Doulton Collectors Fair
The Queensway Hall
Civic Centre
Dunstable, Bedfordshire

Stafford International Doulton Fair
Stafford County Showground
Stafford

Doulton and Beswick Collectors Fair
National Motorcycle Museum
Meriden, Birmingham

Antique Markets

Portobello Road Market
London W11
Saturday only

New Caledonian Market
Bermondsey Square
London SE1
Friday morning

Alfie's Antique Market
13-25 Church Street
London NW8
Tuesday-Saturday

Camden Passage Market
(of Upper Street)
London N1
Wednesday and Saturday

The Potteries Antique Centre
271 Waterloo Road
Cobridge, Stoke-on-Trent, Staffordshire ST6 3HR
Seven days a week

U.S.A.
Auction Houses

Phillips New York
406 East 79th Street
New York, NY 10021

Antique Fairs

Florida Doulton Convention
Guest Quarters Suite Hotel
Cypress Creek
555 NW 62nd Street
Fort Lauderdale, Florida 33309

Doulton Show
Sheraton Poste House
Cherry Hill, New Jersey

Strongsville Pottery and Porcelain Show
Holiday Inn
Strongsville, Ohio

CANADA
Auction Houses

Ritchies
288 King Street East
Toronto, Ontario, M5A 1K4

Antique Shows

Canadian Doulton & Beswick Show and Sale
The Toronto Airport Hilton
5875 Airport Road
Mississauga, Ontario

Antique Markets

Harbourfront Antique Market
390 Queen's Quay West
Toronto, Ontario
(Tuesday - Sunday)

PLACES TO VISIT

John Beswick Factory Tour
Gold Street
Longton, Stoke-on-Trent
ST3 2JP
For opening times and tour information telephone
(0782) 292292

Royal Doulton Factory Tour
and Sir Henry Doulton Gallery
Nile Street
Burslem, Stoke-on-Trent
For opening times and tour information telephone
(0782) 744766

CLUBS AND SOCIETIES

The Royal Doulton International Collectors Club was founded in 1980 to provide an information service on all aspects of the company's products, past and present. The club's magazine, *Gallery*, is published four times a year, and local branches also publish newsletters. There are also several regional groups in the U.S.A. that meet for lectures and other events, and some publish newsletters. Contact the U.S.A. branch for further information.

Headquarters and U.K. Branch

Royal Doulton
Minton House
London Road
Stoke-on-Trent   ST4 7QD

Australian Branch

Royal Doulton Australia Pty Ltd.
17-23 Merriwa Street
Gordon   NSW 2072

Canadian Branch

Royal Doulton Canada Inc.
850 Progress Road
Scarborough, Ontario   M1H 3C4

New Zealand Branch

Royal Doulton
P.O. Box 2059
Auckland

U.S.A. Branch

Royal Doulton U.S.A. Inc
P.O. Box 1815
Somerset, New Jersey   08873

FURTHER READING

Storybook Figures

Royal Doulton Bunnykins Figures, by Louise Irvine
Bunnykins Collectors Book, by Louise Irvine
Beatrix Potter Figures and Giftware, edited by Louise Irvine
The Beswick Price Guide, by Harvey May

Animals, Figures and Character Jugs

Royal Doulton Figures, by Desmond Eyles, Louise Irvine and Valerie Baynton
The Charlton Standard Catalogue of Royal Doulton Animals, by Jean Dale
The Charlton Standard Catalogue of Royal Doulton Figurines, by Jean Dale
The Charlton Standard Catalogue of Royal Doulton Jugs, by Jean Dale
Collecting Character and Toby Jugs, by Jocelyn Lukins
Collecting Doulton Animals, by Jocelyn Lukins
Doulton Flambé Animals, by Jocelyn Lukins
The Character Jug Collectors Handbook, by Kevin Pearson
The Doulton Figure Collectors Handbook, by Kevin Pearson

General

Discovering Royal Doulton, by Michael Doulton
The Doulton Story, by Paul Atterbury and Louise Irvine
Royal Doulton Series Wares, by Louise Irvine (Vols. 1-4)
Limited Edition Loving Cups and Jugs, by Louise Irvine and Richard Dennis
Doulton for the Collector, by Jocelyn Lukins
Doulton Kingsware Flasks, by Jocelyn Lukins
Doulton Burslem Advertising Wares, by Jocelyn Lukins
Doulton Lambeth Advertising Wares, by Jocelyn Lukins
The Doulton Lambeth Wares, by Desmond Eyles
The Doulton Burslem Wares, by Desmond Eyles
Hannah Barlow, by Peter Rose
George Tinworth, by Peter Rose
Sir Henry Doulton Biography, by Edmund Gosse
Phillips Collectors Guide, by Catherine Braithwaite
Royal Doulton, by Jennifer Queree
Collecting Doulton Magazine, published by Francis Joseph, edited by Doug Pinchin

ALICE IN WONDERLAND

2476
ALICE™

Designer:	Albert Hallam and Graham Tongue
Height:	4 3/4", 12.1 cm
Colour:	Blue dress, white apron and red trim
Issued:	1973 - 1983

Beswick Number	Price			
	U.S. $	Can. $	U.K. £	Aust. $
2476	475.00	650.00	245.00	700.00

2477
WHITE RABBIT™

Designer:	Graham Tongue
Height:	4 3/4", 12.1 cm
Colour:	Brown coat, yellow waistcoat
Issued:	1973 - 1983

Beswick Number	Price			
	U.S. $	Can. $	U.K. £	Aust. $
2477	450.00	525.00	245.00	700.00

2478
MOCK TURTLE™

Designer:	Graham Tongue
Height:	4 1/4", 10.8 cm
Colour:	Browns and grey
Issued:	1973 - 1983

Beswick Number	Price			
	U.S. $	Can. $	U.K. £	Aust. $
2478	300.00	400.00	125.00	200.00

2479
MAD HATTER™

Designer: Albert Hallam
Height: 4 1/4", 10.8 cm
Colour: Burgundy coat, yellow and blue checked trousers, yellow and red bowtie, grey hat
Issued: 1973 - 1983

Beswick Number	Price			
	U.S. $	Can. $	U.K. £	Aust. $
2479	375.00	425.00	175.00	700.00

2480
CHESHIRE CAT™

Designer: Albert Hallam and Graham Tongue
Height: 1 1/2", 3.8 cm
Colour: Tabby
Issued: 1973 - 1982

Beswick Number	Price			
	U.S. $	Can. $	U.K. £	Aust. $
2480	650.00	850.00	425.00	950.00

2485
GRYPHON™

Designer: Albert Hallam
Height: 3 1/4", 8.3 cm
Colour: Browns and greens
Issued: 1973 - 1983

Beswick Number	Price			
	U.S. $	Can. $	U.K. £	Aust. $
2485	275.00	325.00	100.00	200.00

2489
KING OF HEARTS™

Designer:	Graham Tongue
Height:	3 3/4", 9.5 cm
Colour:	Burgundy, yellow, white, blue and green
Issued:	1973 - 1983

Beswick Number	Price			
	U.S. $	Can. $	U.K. £	Aust. $
2489	125.00	140.00	55.00	200.00

ALICE SERIES
"King of Hearts"
BESWICK
MADE IN ENGLAND
© ROYAL DOULTON TABLEWARE LTE.
REGISTRATION APPLIED FOR

2490
QUEEN OF HEARTS™

Designer:	Graham Tongue
Height:	4", 10.1 cm
Colour:	Blue, green, yellow, white and burgundy
Issued:	1973 - 1983

Beswick Number	Price			
	U.S. $	Can. $	U.K. £	Aust. $
2490	125.00	140.00	55.00	200.00

ALICE SERIES
"Queen of Hearts"
BESWICK
MADE IN ENGLAND
© ROYAL DOULTON TABLEWARE LTD. 1973
REGISTRATION APPLIED FOR

2545
DODO™

Designer:	David Lyttleton
Height:	4", 10.1 cm
Colour:	Browns and greens
Issued:	1975 - 1983

Beswick Number	Price			
	U.S. $	Can. $	U.K. £	Aust. $
2545	325.00	450.00	135.00	400.00

ALICE SERIES
"Dodo"
BESWICK
MADE IN ENGLAND
© ROYAL DOULTON TABLEWARE LTD. 1975
REGISTRATION APPLIED FOR

2546
FISH FOOTMAN™

Designer: David Lyttleton
Height: 4 3/4", 14.6 cm
Colour: Blue, gold, white and brown
Issued: 1975 - 1983

Beswick		*Price*		
Number	*U.S. $*	*Can. $*	*U.K. £*	*Aust. $*
2546	325.00	450.00	160.00	500.00

2547
FROG FOOTMAN™

Designer: David Lyttleton
Height: 4 1/4", 10.8 cm
Colour: Maroon jacket with yellow
trim and blue trousers
Issued: 1975 - 1983

Beswick		*Price*		
Number	*U.S. $*	*Can. $*	*U.K. £*	*Aust. $*
2547	325.00	450.00	190.00	450.00

BEATRIX POTTER FIGURES

BEATRIX POTTER BACKSTAMPS

BP-1. BESWICK GOLD CIRCLE
ISSUED 1948 TO 1954

BP-1 was used on 21 figures between 1948 and 1954. There are two varieties of this backstamp, the first a circle and the second a modification of the circle. The modification was necessary due to the small base on two figures - Mrs. Rabbit and the Tailor of Gloucester. The backstamp circle was flattened and the copyright was written in script lettering.

The following is a list of figures that can be found with a BP-1 backstamp:

Benjamin Bunny, first version
Flopsy, Mopsy and Cottontail
Foxy Whiskered Gentleman
Hunca Munca
Jemima Puddleduck
Johnny Townmouse
Lady Mouse
Little Pig Robinson, first variation
Miss Moppet, first variation
Mr. Jeremy Fisher, first version
Mrs. Rabbit, first version
Mrs. Tiggy Winkle, first and
    second variations
Mrs. Tittlemouse
Peter Rabbit, first version
Ribby
Samuel Whiskers
Squirrel Nutkin, first variation
Tailor of Gloucester, first version
Timmy Tiptoes, first variation
Timmy Willie From Johnny Town-Mouse
Tom Kitten, first version

BP-1 Bewsick Gold Circle

BP-2. BESWICK GOLD OVAL
ISSUED 1952 TO 1972

The gold oval was in use for 18 years, between 1955 and 1972, and it was used on 38 figures. Pig-Wig, introduced in 1972, was the last in line for the gold oval backstamp, and in some quarters they still doubt that it officially exists.

The following is a list of figures that can be found with a BP-2 backstamp:

Amiable Guinea Pig
Anna Maria
Appley Dappley, first and second version
Aunt Pettitoes
Benjamin Bunny, first version
Cecily Parsley, first version
Cousin Ribby
Duches (with flowers)
Flopsy, Mopsy and Cottontail
Foxy Whiskered Gentleman
Goody Tiptoes
Hunca Munca
Jemima Puddleduck
Johnny Townmouse
Lady Mouse
Little Pig Robinson, first variation
Miss Moppet, first variation
Mr. Benjamin Bunny, first version
Mr. Jeremy Fisher, first variation
Mrs. Flopsy Bunny
Mrs. Rabbit, first version
Mrs. Tiggy Winkle, first and second variation
Mrs. Tittlemouse
Old Mr. Brown
Old Woman Who Lived in a Shoe
Peter Rabbit, first version
Pickles
Pigling Bland, first variation
Pig-Wig
Ribby
Samuel Whiskers
Squirrel Nutkin, first variation
Tabitha Twitchit, first variation
Tailor of Gloucester, first version
Timmy Tiptoes, first variation
Timmy Willie From Johnny Town-Mouse
Tom Kitten, first version
Tommy Brock, first and second version

BP-2 Beswick Gold Oval

BP-3. BESWICK BROWN LINE
ISSUED 1973 TO 1988

In use between 1973 and 1988, these brown line backstamps (Beswick and England are in a straight line) appear on 69 figures, including the different versions. The brown line backstamp saw three major revisions during the 16 years it was in use.

BP-3a — Potter's, no date, issued 1973 to 1974
(no copyright date)

BP-3b — Potter's, date, issued 1974 to 1985
(copyright date)

BP-3c — Potter, date, issued 1985 to 1988
(no "s" on Potter)

BP-4. BESWICK SIGNATURE
ISSUED 1988 TO 1989

This era saw the Beswick backstamp converted to the Royal Doulton backstamp. The connection with Beswick was kept by the addition of the John Beswick signature to the backstamp. In use for a year to a year and a half, this is one of the shortest time periods for a backstamp.

BP-5. ROYAL ALBERT GOLD CROWN
ISSUED 1989

The gold backstamp was reinstituted for 1989 to mark the change from the Doulton/Beswick backstamps to Royal Albert. It was used on only the following six figures:

    Benjamin Bunny
    Flopsy, Mopsy and Cottontail
    Hunca Munca
    Jemima Puddleduck
    Mrs. Rabbit and Bunnies
    Peter Rabbit

BP-6. ROYAL ALBERT BROWN CROWN - SMALL
ISSUED 1989 TO DATE

There are two known varieties of this backstamp with and without the crown.

BP-7. ROYAL ALBERT CROWN - LARGE
ISSUED 1993 TO DATE

Issued on the large size Beatrix Potter figures this category has three different divisions:

BP-7a Royal Albert Brown Crown
BP-7b 100th Anniversary of Peter Rabbit 1893-1993
BP-7c 100th Anniversary of The Beswick Studio 1894-1994

AMIABLE GUINEA PIG™

Modeller: Albert Hallam
Height: 3 1/2", 8.9 cm
Colour: Tan jacket, white waistcoat, yellow trousers
Issued: 1967 - 1983

Back Stamp	Beswick Number	Doulton Number	U.S. $	Price Can. $	U.K. £	Aust. $
BP-2	2061	P2061	600.00	775.00	350.00	950.00
BP-3a			325.00	550.00	250.00	750.00
BP-3b			300.00	500.00	225.00	700.00

Note: The colour of the coat varies from tan to brown.

AND THIS PIG HAD NONE™

Modeller: Martyn Alcock
Height: 4", 10.1 cm
Colour: Mauve dress, mottled burgundy and green shawl, brown hat
Issued: 1992 to the present

Back Stamp	Beswick Number	Doulton Number	U.S. $	Price Can. $	U.K. £	Aust. $
BP-6	3319	P3319	32.50	—	14.95	60.00

ANNA MARIA™

Modeller: Albert Hallam
Height: 3", 7.6 cm
Colour: Blue dress and white apron
Issued: 1963 - 1983

Back Stamp	Beswick Number	Doulton Number	U.S. $	Price Can. $	U.K. £	Aust. $
BP-2	1851	P1851	525.00	550.00	250.00	600.00
BP-3a			275.00	375.00	175.00	400.00
BP-3b			225.00	325.00	150.00	350.00

Note: Dress is bright blue in earlier versions and pale blue in later versions.

APPLEY DAPPLY™
First Version (Bottle Out)

Modeller:	Albert Hallam
Height:	3 1/4", 8.3 cm
Colour:	Brown mouse, white apron, blue trim, blue bow, yellow basket, tray of jam tarts
Issued:	1971 - 1975

Back Stamp	Beswick Number	Doulton Number	U.S. $	Price Can. $	U.K. £	Aust. $
BP-2	2333	P2333/1	750.00	900.00	400.00	950.00
BP-3a			400.00	500.00	250.00	350.00
BP-3b			375.00	450.00	200.00	300.00

APPLEY DAPPLY™
Second Version (Bottle In)

Modeller:	Albert Hallam
Height:	3 1/4", 8.3 cm
Colour:	Brown mouse, white apron, blue trim, blue bow, yellow basket, tray of jam tarts
Issued:	1975 to the present

Back Stamp	Beswick Number	Doulton Number	U.S. $	Price Can. $	U.K. £	Aust. $
BP-3b	2333	P2333/2	80.00	110.00	50.00	100.00
BP-3c			110.00	150.00	75.00	150.00
BP-6			32.50	50.00	14.95	60.00

AUNT PETTITOES™

Modeller:	Albert Hallam
Height:	3 3/4", 9.5 cm
Colour:	Blue dress and white cap with blue polka dots
Issued:	1970 - 1993

Back Stamp	Beswick Number	Doulton Number	U.S. $	Price Can. $	U.K. £	Aust. $
BP-2	2276	P2276	450.00	550.00	250.00	500.00
BP-3a			95.00	135.00	65.00	150.00
BP-3b			75.00	90.00	50.00	100.00
BP-3c			95.00	135.00	65.00	150.00
BP-6			45.00	50.00	30.00	75.00

Note: The dress is light blue in earlier versions and bright blue in later versions.

BABBITTY BUMBLE™

Modeller: Warren Platt
Height: 2 3/4", 7.0 cm
Colour: Black and gold
Issued: 1989 - 1993

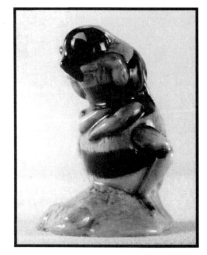

Back Stamp	Beswick Number	Doulton Number	U.S. $	Price Can. $	U.K. £	Aust. $
BP-6	2971	P2971	75.00	100.00	40.00	90.00

BENJAMIN ATE A LETTUCE LEAF™

Modeller: Martyn Alcock
Height: 4 3/4", 11.9 cm
Colour: Brown, white and yellow
Issued: 1992 to the present

Back Stamp	Beswick Number	Doulton Number	U.S. $	Price Can. $	U.K. £	Aust. $
BP-6	3317	P3317	32.50	—	14.95	65.00

BENJAMIN BUNNY™
First Version (Ears Out, Shoes Out)

Modeller: Arthur Gredington
Height: 4", 10.1 cm
Colour: Variation No. 1 — pale green jacket
Variation No. 2 — brown jacket
Issued: 1948 - 1974

Back Stamp	Beswick Number	Colour Variation	U.S. $	Price Can. $	U.K. £	Aust. $
BP-1	1105/1	Pale green	500.00	600.00	325.00	550.00
BP-2		Pale green	450.00	550.00	300.00	500.00
BP-2		Brown	450.00	550.00	300.00	500.00
BP-3a		Pale green	325.00	450.00	225.00	375.00
BP-3b		Brown	275.00	400.00	200.00	325.00

BENJAMIN BUNNY™
Second Version (Ears Out, Shoes In)

Modeller:	Arthur Gredington
Height:	4", 10.1 cm
Colour:	Variation No. 1 — pale green jacket
	Variation No. 2 — brown jacket
Issued:	1972 - c.1980

Back Stamp	Beswick Number	Colour Variation	U.S. $	Can. $	U.K. £	Aust. $
BP-2	1105/2	Pale green	450.00	500.00	300.00	550.00
BP-3a		Pale green	300.00	400.00	275.00	375.00
BP-3a		Brown	300.00	400.00	275.00	375.00
BP-3b		Pale green	250.00	350.00	250.00	325.00
BP-3b		Brown	250.00	350.00	250.00	325.00

BENJAMIN BUNNY™
Third Version (Ears In, Shoes In)

Modeller:	Arthur Gredington
Height:	4", 10.1 cm
Colour:	Brown jacket, green beret
	with orange pompon
Issued:	c.1980 to the present

Back Stamp	Beswick Number	Doulton Number	U.S. $	Can. $	U.K. £	Aust. $
BP-3b	1105/3	P1105/3	75.00	100.00	50.00	60.00
BP-3c			95.00	115.00	65.00	100.00
BP-4			75.00	95.00	75.00	100.00
BP-5			125.00	150.00	50.00	175.00
BP-6			32.50	50.00	14.95	60.00

BENJAMIN BUNNY™
Fourth Version (Large)

Modeller:	Martyn Alcock
Height:	6 1/4", 15.9 cm
Colour:	Tan jacket, green beret
	with orange pompon
Issued:	1994 to the present

Back Stamp	Beswick Number	Doulton Number	U.S. $	Can. $	U.K.£	Aust. $
BP-7	3403	P3403	72.50	96.00	27.95	129.00

BENJAMIN BUNNY SAT ON A BANK™
First Version (Head Looks Down)

Modeller: David Lyttleton
Height: 3 3/4", 9.5 cm
Colour: Brown jacket
Issued: 1983 - 1983

Back Stamp	Beswick Number	Doulton Number	U.S. $	Price Can. $	U.K. £	Aust. $
BP-3b	2803/1	P2803/1	125.00	150.00	95.00	165.00

BENJAMIN BUNNY SAT ON A BANK™
Second Version (Head Looks Up)

Modeller: David Lyttleton
Height: 3 3/4", 9.5 cm
Colour: Golden brown jacket
Issued: 1983 to the present

Back Stamp	Beswick Number	Doulton Number	U.S. $	Price Can. $	U.K. £	Aust. $
BP-3b	2803/2	P2803/2	125.00	150.00	95.00	165.00
BP-3c			160.00	195.00	110.00	195.00
BP-6			32.50	—	14.95	57.00

BENJAMIN WAKES UP™

Modeller: Amanda Hughes-Lubeck
Height: 2 1/4", 5.7 cm
Colour: Green, white and orange
Issued: 1991 to the present

Back Stamp	Beswick Number	Doulton Number	U.S. $	Price Can. $	U.K. £	Aust. $
BP-6	3234	P3234	32.50	—	14.95	65.00

CECILY PARSLEY™
First Version (Blue Dress, Head Down)

Modeller:	Arthur Gredington
Height:	4", 10.1 cm
Colour:	Bright blue dress, white apron, brown pail
Issued:	1965 - 1985

Back Stamp	Beswick Number	Doulton Number	U.S. $	Price Can. $	U.K. £	Aust. $
BP-2	1941/1	P1941/1	275.00	350.00	150.00	350.00
BP-3a			110.00	125.00	55.00	125.00
BP-3b			85.00	100.00	45.00	100.00
BP-3c			110.00	125.00	55.00	125.00

CECILY PARSLEY™
Second Version (Pale Blue Dress, Head Up)

Modeller:	Arthur Gredington
Height:	4", 10.1 cm
Colour:	Pale blue dress, white apron
Issued:	1985 - 1993

Back Stamp	Beswick Number	Doulton Number	U.S. $	Price Can. $	U.K. £	Aust. $
BP-3c	1941/2	P1941/2	125.00	150.00	45.00	100.00
BP-6			45.00	65.00	30.00	65.00

CHIPPY HACKEE™

Modeller:	David Lyttleton
Height:	3 3/4"
Colour:	Pale green blanket, white handkerchief, green foot bath
Issued:	1979 - 1993

Back Stamp	Beswick Number	Doulton Number	U.S. $	Price Can. $	U.K. £	Aust. $
BP-3b	2627	P2627	85.00	110.00	45.00	120.00
BP-3c			115.00	150.00	65.00	150.00
BP-6			45.00	65.00	30.00	65.00

Note: The colour of the blanket may range from pale green to pale yellow.

CHRISTMAS STOCKING™

Modeller:	Martyn Alcock
Height:	3 1/4", 8.3 cm
Colour:	Brown mice, red and white striped stocking
Issued:	1991 - 1994

Back Stamp	Beswick Number	Doulton Number	U.S. $	Price Can. $	U.K. £	Aust. $
BP-6	3257	P3257	95.00	115.00	45.00	85.00

COTTONTAIL™

Modeller:	David Lyttleton
Height:	3 3/4", 9.5 cm
Colour:	Blue dress, brown chair
Issued:	1985 - 1996

Back Stamp	Beswick Number	Doulton Number	U.S. $	Price Can. $	U.K.£	Aust. $
BP-3b	2878	P2878	60.00	75.00	40.00	75.00
BP-3c			90.00	110.00	65.00	110.00
BP-6			32.50	57.00	14.95	60.00

COUSIN RIBBY™

Modeller:	Albert Hallam
Height:	3 1/2", 8.9 cm
Colour:	Pink skirt and hat, green apron, blue shawl, yellow basket
Issued:	1970 - 1993

Back Stamp	Beswick Number	Doulton Number	U.S. $	Price Can. $	U.K. £	Aust. $
BP-2	2284	P2284	450.00	525.00	275.00	550.00
BP-3a			100.00	135.00	70.00	135.00
BP-3b			65.00	90.00	45.00	90.00
BP-3c			100.00	135.00	70.00	135.00
BP-6			55.00	65.00	30.00	70.00

DIGGORY DIGGORY DELVET™

Modeller:	David Lyttleton
Height:	2 3/4", 7 cm
Colour:	Grey mole
Issued:	1982 to the present

BEATRIX POTTER
"Diggory Diggory Delvet"
© Frederick Warne & Co. 1982
Licensed by Copyrights
BESWICK ENGLAND

Back Stamp	Beswick Number	Doulton Number	U.S. $	Price Can. $	U.K. £	Aust. $
BP-3b	2713	P2713	70.00	100.00	50.00	150.00
BP-3c			90.00	125.00	70.00	175.00
BP-6			32.50	—	14.95	75.00

DUCHESS™
Style One (Holding Flowers)

Modeller:	Graham Orwell
Height:	3 3/4", 9.5 cm
Colour:	Black dog, multi-coloured flowers
Issued:	1955 - 1967

Back Stamp	Beswick Number	Doulton Number	U.S. $	Price Can. $	U.K. £	Aust. $
BP-2	1355	P1355	2,500.00	3,000.00	1,500.00	3,000.00

Note: The above italized prices for this rare figure are indications only, and the actual selling price may be higher or lower, depending on market conditions.

DUCHESS™
Style Two (Holding a Pie)

Modeller:	Graham Tongue
Height:	4", 10.1 cm
Colour:	Black dog, blue bow, light brown pie
Issued:	1979 - 1982

BEATRIX POTTER'S
"Duchess"
F. Warne & Co. Ltd.
© Copyright 1979
BESWICK ENGLAND

Back Stamp	Beswick Number	Doulton Number	U.S. $	Price Can. $	U.K. £	Aust. $
BP-3b	2601	P2601	300.00	400.00	225.00	350.00

FIERCE BAD RABBIT™
First Version (Feet Out)

Modeller: David Lyttleton
Height: 4 3/4", 12.1 cm
Colour: Dark brown and white rabbit,
red-brown carrot, green seat
Issued: 1977 - 1980

Back Stamp	Beswick Number	Doulton Number	U.S. $	Price Can. $	U.K. £	Aust. $
BP-3b	2586/1	P2586/1	175.00	325.00	145.00	350.00

FIERCE BAD RABBIT™
Second Version (Feet In)

Modeller: David Lyttleton
Height: 4 3/4", 12.1 cm
Colour: Light brown and white rabbit,
red-brown carrot, green seat
Issued: 1980 to the present

Back Stamp	Beswick Number	Doulton Number	U.S. $	Price Can. $	U.K. £	Aust. $
BP-3b	2586/2	P2586/2	95.00	125.00	65.00	125.00
BP-3c			125.00	150.00	85.00	150.00
BP-4			95.00	125.00	50.00	125.00
BP-6			32.50	50.00	14.95	75.00

FLOPSY, MOPSY AND COTTONTAIL™

Modeller: Arthur Gredington
Height: 2 1/2", 6.4 cm
Colour: Brown and white rabbits
wearing rose-pink cloaks
Issued: 1954 to the present

Back Stamp	Beswick Number	Doulton Number	U.S. $	Price Can. $	U.K. £	Aust. $
BP-1	1274	P1274	400.00	450.00	200.00	500.00
BP-2			275.00	300.00	110.00	425.00
BP-3a			110.00	135.00	75.00	135.00
BP-3b			75.00	90.00	55.00	90.00
BP-3c			110.00	135.00	75.00	135.00
BP-4			85.00	100.00	50.00	100.00
BP-5			150.00	175.00	95.00	175.00
BP-6			32.50	50.00	14.95	65.00

Note: Three colour variations of the cloaks exist, beginning with orange,
then rose-pink and finally pink.

FOXY READING COUNTRY NEWS™

Modeller:	Amanda Hughes-Lubeck
Height:	4 1/4", 10.8 cm
Colour:	Brown and green
Issued:	1990 to the present

Back Stamp	Beswick Number	Doulton Number	U.S. $	Price Can. $	U.K. £	Aust. $
BP-6	3219	P3219	55.00	—	21.00	110.00

FOXY WHISKERED GENTLEMAN™
First Version

Modeller:	Arthur Gredington
Height:	4 3/4", 12.1 cm
Colour:	Pale green jacket and trousers, pink waistcoat
Issued:	1954 to the present

Back Stamp	Beswick Number	Doulton Number	U.S. $	Price Can. $	U.K. £	Aust. $
BP-1	1277	P1277	400.00	450.00	250.00	500.00
BP-2			300.00	350.00	150.00	350.00
BP-3a			125.00	175.00	85.00	175.00
BP-3b			95.00	135.00	60.00	135.00
BP-3c			125.00	175.00	85.00	175.00
BP-4			85.00	135.00	75.00	150.00
BP-6			32.50	—	14.95	65.00

Note: Variations occur with the head looking either right or left.

FOXY WHISKERED GENTLEMAN™
Second Version (Large Size)

Modeller:	Arthur Gredington
Height:	6", 15 cm
Colour:	Pale green jacket and trousers, pink waistcoat
Issued:	1995 to the present

Back Stamp	Beswick Number	Doulton Number	U.S. $	Price Can. $	U.K. £	Aust. $
BP-7	3450	P3450	72.50	96.00	27.95	129.00

GENTLEMAN MOUSE MADE A BOW™

Modeller: Ted Chawner
Height: 3", 7.6 cm
Colour: Brown, blue and white
Issued: 1990 - 1996

Back Stamp	Beswick Number	Doulton Number	U.S. $	Price Can. $	U.K. £	Aust. $
BP-6	3200	P3200	32.50	—	14.95	80.00

GINGER™

Modeller: David Lyttleton
Height: 3 3/4", 9.5 cm
Colour: Green, white and brown
Issued: 1976 - 1982

Back Stamp	Beswick Number	Doulton Number	U.S. $	Price Can. $	U.K. £	Aust. $
BP-3b	2559	P2559	800.00	1,000.00	475.00	700.00

Note: The jacket colour varies from light to dark green.

GOODY TIPTOES™

Modeller: Arthur Gredington
Height: 3 1/2", 8.9 cm
Colour: Grey squirrel wearing pink dress and white apron, brown sack with yellow nuts
Issued: 1961 to the present

Back Stamp	Beswick Number	Doulton Number	U.S. $	Price Can. $	U.K. £	Aust. $
BP-2	1675	P1675	300.00	375.00	175.00	350.00
BP-3a			95.00	115.00	65.00	125.00
BP-3b			65.00	80.00	40.00	90.00
BP-3c			95.00	115.00	65.00	125.00
BP-6			32.50	50.00	14.95	69.00

Note: Goody Tiptoes was issued with two different bases and her dress varies from light to deep pink.

GOODY AND TIMMY TIPTOES™

Modeller:	David Lyttleton
Height:	4", 10.1 cm
Colour:	Timmy - rose coat
	Goody - pink overdress with green and biege underskirt, green umbrella
Issued:	1986 - 1996

BEATRIX POTTER
"Goody & Timmy Tiptoes"
© Frederick Warne & Co. 1986
Licensed by Copyrights
BESWICK ENGLAND

Back Stamp	Beswick Number	Doulton Number	U.S. $	Price Can. $	U.K. £	Aust. $
BP-3c	2957	P2957	225.00	300.00	150.00	300.00
BP-6			55.00	93.00	24.95	90.00

HUNCA MUNCA™

Modeller:	Arthur Gredington
Height:	2 3/4", 7 cm
Colour:	Blue dress, white apron, pink blanket and straw cradle
Issued:	1951 to the present

BEATRIX POTTER'S
"HUNCA MUNCA"
F. WARNE & CO. LTD.
COPYRIGHT

Back Stamp	Beswick Number	Doulton Number	U.S. $	Price Can. $	U.K. £	Aust. $
BP-1	1198	P1198	300.00	350.00	125.00	350.00
BP-2			250.00	300.00	100.00	325.00
BP-3a			125.00	150.00	90.00	150.00
BP-3b			85.00	110.00	65.00	110.00
BP-3c			125.00	150.00	90.00	150.00
BP-4			85.00	135.00	75.00	145.00
BP-5			130.00	160.00	50.00	160.00
BP-6			32.50	50.00	14.95	65.00

HUNCA MUNCA SPILLS THE BEADS™

Modeller:	Martyn Alcock
Height:	3 1/4", 8.3 cm
Colour:	Brown mouse, blue and white rice jar
Issued:	1992 - 1996

ROYAL ALBERT ®
ENGLAND
Hunca Munca
spills the beads
Beatrix Potter
© F WARNE & CO 1991
© 1992 ROYAL ALBERT LTD

Back Stamp	Beswick Number	Doulton Number	U.S. $	Price Can. $	U.K. £	Aust. $
BP-6	3288	P3288	32.50	—	15.95	70.00

HUNCA MUNCA SWEEPING™

Modeller:	David Lyttleton
Height:	3 1/2", 8.9 cm
Colour:	Mauve patterned dress with white apron, green broom handle
Issued:	1977 to the present

BEATRIX POTTER'S
"Hunca Munca Sweeping"
F. Warne & Co.Ltd.
© Copyright 1977
BESWICK ENGLAND

Back Stamp	Beswick Number	Doulton Number	U.S. $	Price Can. $	U.K. £	Aust. $
BP-3b	2584	P2584	95.00	130.00	65.00	175.00
BP-3c			130.00	175.00	90.00	220.00
BP-4			85.00	160.00	85.00	175.00
BP-6			32.50	50.00	14.95	60.00

JEMIMA PUDDLE-DUCK™
First Version (Small Size)

Modeller:	Arthur Gredington
Height:	4 3/4", 12.1 cm
Colour:	White duck, mauve or pink shawl, light blue bonnet
Issued:	1948 to the present

BEATRIX POTTER'S
Jemima Puddleduck

Back Stamp	Beswick Number	Doulton Number	U.S. $	Price Can. $	U.K. £	Aust. $
BP-1	1092/1	P1092/1	275.00	325.00	125.00	350.00
BP-2			225.00	250.00	100.00	300.00
BP-3a			100.00	130.00	90.00	140.00
BP-3b			75.00	90.00	65.00	100.00
BP-3c			100.00	130.00	90.00	140.00
BP-4			85.00	110.00	50.00	125.00
BP-5			130.00	160.00	90.00	185.00
BP-6			32.50	50.00	14.95	69.00

JEMIMA PUDDLE-DUCK™
Second Version (Large Size)

Modeller:	Arthur Gredington
Height:	6", 15 cm
Colour:	White duck, mauve shawl, light blue bonnet
Issued:	1993 to the present

Beswick Ware
MADE IN ENGLAND
BEATRIX POTTER'S
JEMIMA PUDDLE-DUCK
BESWICK CENTENARY
1894-1994
© F.WARNE & CO.1993
© 1993 ROYAL DOULTON

Back Stamp	Beswick Number	Doulton Number	U.S. $	Price Can. $	U.K. £	Aust. $
BP-7a	1092/2	P1092/2	72.50	96.00	27.95	129.00
BP-7c	Beswick Centenary		95.00	125.00	50.00	150.00

JEMIMA PUDDLE-DUCK WITH FOXY WHISKERED GENTLEMAN™

Modeller:	Ted Chawner
Height:	4 3/4", 12.1 cm
Colour:	Brown, green, white and blue
Issued:	1990 to the present

ROYAL ALBERT ®
ENGLAND
Jemima Puddleduck with
Foxy Whiskered Gentleman
Beatrix Potter
© F WARNE & CO 1989
© 1989 ROYAL ALBERT LTD

Back Stamp	Beswick Number	Doulton Number	U.S. $	Price Can. $	U.K. £	Aust. $
BP-6	3193	P3193	55.00	—	24.95	100.00

JEMIMA PUDDLE-DUCK MADE A FEATHER NEST™

Modeller:	David Lyttleton
Height:	2 1/4", 5.7 cm
Colour:	Blue hat, mauve or pink shawl, white duck
Issued:	1983 to the present

BEATRIX POTTER'S
Jemima Puddleduck
Made a feather nest
© Frederick Warne P.L.C. 1983
BESWICK
ENGLAND

Back Stamp	Beswick Number	Doulton Number	U.S. $	Price Can. $	U.K. £	Aust. $
BP-3b	2823	P2823	65.00	80.00	40.00	100.00
BP-3c			95.00	115.00	65.00	135.00
BP-4			85.00	110.00	50.00	125.00
BP-6			32.50	—	14.95	60.00

Note: This model was issued with either a mauve or pink shawl.

JOHN JOINER™

Modeller:	Graham Tongue
Height:	2 1/2", 6.4 cm
Colour:	Brown dog wearing green jacket
Issued:	1990 to the present

ROYAL ALBERT ®
ENGLAND
John Joiner
Beatrix Potter
© F. WARNE & CO. 1990
© 1990 ROYAL ALBERT LTD

Back Stamp	Beswick Number	Doulton Number	U.S. $	Price Can. $	U.K. £	Aust. $
BP-6	2965	P2965	32.50	—	14.95	80.00

JEMIMA PUDDLE-DUCK™

Large Size   Wall Plaque   Gold Backstamp   Character Jug

DISPLAY STAND
Pig-Wig™   Simpkin™   Duchess™   Ginger™ Amiable Guinea Pig™

TIMMY TIPTOES™
First Version   Second Version

SQUIRREL NUTKIN™
First Version   Second Version

TOM KITTEN™
First Version   Second Version

PETER RABBIT™
First Version   Second Version

APPLEY DAPPLY™

First Version   Second Version

MRS. TIGGY WINKLE™

First Version   Second Version on a Tree Lamp Base

TOMMY BROCK™

Spade Out   Spade In

MR. BENJAMIN BUNNY™

First Version   Second Version

MISS MOPPET™
First Version   Second Version

TABITHA TWITCHIT™
First Version   Second Version

LITTLE PIG ROBINSON™
First Version   Second Version

PIGLING BLAND™
First Version   Second Version

FIERCE BAD RABBIT™
First Version   Second Version

BENJAMIN BUNNY SAT ON A BANK™
First Version   Second Version

MR. JEREMY FISHER™
First Version   Second Version

MR. JACKSON™
First Version   Second Version

BENJAMIN BUNNY™

First Version   Second Version   Third Version

MRS. RABBIT™   **CECILEY PARSLEY™**

First Version   Second Version   First Version   Second Version

TOM KITTEN™

| Character Jug | Large Size | First Version | Second Version |

PETER RABBIT™

| Large Size | First Version | Second Version | Character Jug |

TOMMY BROCK™

First Version   Second Version   Third Version   Fourth Version

DUCHESS™

Style Two   Style One

JOHNNY TOWN-MOUSE™

Modeller:	Arthur Gredington
Height:	3 1/2", 8.9 cm
Colour:	Pale blue jacket, white and brown waistcoat
Issued:	1954 - 1993

Back Stamp	Beswick Number	Doulton Number	U.S. $	Price Can. $	U.K. £	Aust. $
BP-1	1276	P1276	275.00	350.00	135.00	400.00
BP-2			225.00	250.00	100.00	275.00
BP-3a			100.00	125.00	60.00	150.00
BP-3b			65.00	90.00	45.00	110.00
BP-3c			100.00	125.00	60.00	150.00
BP-6			50.00	65.00	30.00	65.00

Note: Jacket colouring varies from pale to deep blue.

JOHNNY TOWN-MOUSE WITH BAG™

Modeller:	Ted Chawner
Height:	3 1/2", 8.9 cm
Colour:	Light brown coat and hat, yellow-cream waistcoat
Issued:	1988 - 1994

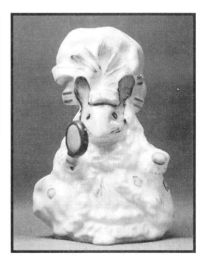

Back Stamp	Beswick Number	Doulton Number	U.S. $	Price Can. $	U.K. £	Aust. $
BP-4	3094	P3094	260.00	390.00	185.00	425.00
BP-6			100.00	115.00	35.00	70.00

LADY MOUSE™

Modeller:	Arthur Gredington
Height:	4", 10.1 cm
Colour:	White dress with yellow trim and blue polka-dot sleeves, white hat with purple and blue highlights
Issued:	1950 to the present

Back Stamp	Beswick Number	Doulton Number	U.S. $	Price Can. $	U.K. £	Aust. $
BP-1	1183	P1183	325.00	375.00	150.00	400.00
BP-2			275.00	300.00	110.00	350.00
BP-3a			100.00	215.00	80.00	160.00
BP-3b			75.00	175.00	55.00	125.00
BP-3c			100.00	215.00	80.00	160.00
BP-6			32.50	—	14.95	69.00

LADY MOUSE MADE A CURTSEY™

Modeller:	Amanda Hughes-Lubeck
Height:	3 1/4", 8.3 cm
Colour:	Purple-pink and white
Issued:	1990 to the present

Back Stamp	Beswick Number	Doulton Number	U.S. $	Price Can. $	U.K. £	Aust. $
BP-6	3220	P3220	32.50	—	14.95	75.00

LITTLE BLACK RABBIT™

Modeller:	David Lyttleton
Height:	4 1/2", 11.4 cm
Colour:	Black rabbit wearing green waistcoat
Issued:	1977 to the present

Back Stamp	Beswick Number	Doulton Number	U.S. $	Price Can. $	U.K. £	Aust. $
BP-3b	2585	P2585	65.00	90.00	45.00	125.00
BP-3c			95.00	125.00	70.00	150.00
BP-6			32.50	50.00	14.95	90.00

Note: The jacket colouring varies from light to dark green.

LITTLE PIG ROBINSON™
First Variation (Blue Stripes)

Modeller:	Arthur Gredington
Height:	4", 10.2 cm
Colour:	White and blue striped dress, brown basket with yellow cauliflowers
Issued:	1948 - 1974

Back Stamp	Beswick Number	Doulton Number	U.S. $	Price Can. $	U.K. £	Aust. $
BP-1	1104/1	P1104/1	500.00	600.00	275.00	600.00
BP-2			400.00	500.00	225.00	500.00
BP-3a			400.00	500.00	225.00	500.00

LITTLE PIG ROBINSON™
Second Variation (Blue Checked)

Modeller:	Arthur Gredington
Height:	3 1/2", 8.9 cm
Colour:	Blue dress, brown basket with cream cauliflowers
Issued:	c.1974 to the present

Back Stamp	Beswick Number	Doulton Number	U.S. $	Price Can. $	U.K. £	Aust. $
BP-3b	1104/2	P1104/2	75.00	110.00	45.00	115.00
BP-3c			110.00	150.00	75.00	150.00
BP-6			32.50	—	14.95	70.00

LITTLE PIG ROBINSON SPYING™

Modeller:	Ted Chawner
Height:	3 1/2", 8.9 cm
Colour:	Blue and white striped dress, rose-pink chair
Issued:	1987 - 1993

Back Stamp	Beswick Number	Doulton Number	U.S. $	Price Can. $	U.K. £	Aust. $
BP-3c	3031	P3031	250.00	350.00	175.00	350.00
BP-6			90.00	110.00	35.00	90.00

MISS DORMOUSE™

Modeller:	Martyn Alcock
Height:	4", 10.1 cm
Colour:	Blue, white and pink
Issued:	1991 - 1995

Back Stamp	Beswick Number	Doulton Number	U.S. $	Price Can. $	U.K. £	Aust. $
BP-6	3251	P3251	50.00	75.00	30.00	75.00

MISS MOPPET™
First Variation (Mottled Brown Cat)

Modeller:	Arthur Gredington
Height:	3", 7.6 cm
Colour:	Dark brown cat, blue checkered kerchief
Issued:	1954 - c.1978

Back Stamp	Beswick Number	Doulton Number	U.S. $	Price Can. $	U.K. £	Aust. $
BP-1	1275/1	P1275/1	250.00	325.00	150.00	350.00
BP-2			225.00	275.00	100.00	300.00
BP-3a			200.00	250.00	80.00	275.00
BP-3b			200.00	250.00	80.00	275.00

MISS MOPPET™
Second Variation (Brown Striped Cat)

Modeller:	Arthur Gredington
Height:	3", 7.6 cm
Colour:	Light brown cat, blue checkered kerchief
Issued:	1978 to the present

Back Stamp	Beswick Number	Doulton Number	U.S. $	Price Can. $	U.K. £	Aust. $
BP-3b	1275/2	P1275/2	55.00	100.00	45.00	115.00
BP-3c			75.00	125.00	65.00	135.00
BP-6			32.50	50.00	14.95	60.00

MITTENS AND MOPPET™

Modeller:	Ted Chawner
Height:	3 3/4", 9.5 cm
Colour:	Blue, brown and grey
Issued:	1990 - 1994

Back Stamp	Beswick Number	Doulton Number	U.S. $	Price Can. $	U.K. £	Aust. $
BP-6	3197	P3197	60.00	85.00	35.00	85.00

MOTHER LADYBIRD™

Modeller:	Warren Platt
Height:	2 1/2", 6 .4 cm
Colour:	Red and black
Issued:	1989 - 1996

Back Stamp	Beswick Number	Doulton Number	U.S. $	Price Can. $	U.K. £	Aust. $
BP-6	2966	P2966	32.50	—	14.95	75.00

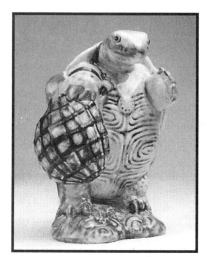

MR. ALDERMAN PTOLEMY™

Modeller:	Graham Tongue
Height:	3 1/2", 8.9 cm
Colour:	Brown, grey and green
Issued:	1973 to the present

Back Stamp	Beswick Number	Doulton Number	U.S. $	Price Can. $	U.K. £	Aust. $
BP-3a	2424	P2424	200.00	235.00	110.00	250.00
BP-3b			175.00	200.00	85.00	225.00
BP-3c			200.00	235.00	110.00	250.00
BP-6			32.50	50.00	14.95	70.00

MR. BENJAMIN BUNNY™
First Version (Pipe Out)

Modeller:	Arthur Gredington
Height:	4 1/4", 10.8 cm
Colour:	Dark maroon jacket, yellow waistcoat
Issued:	1965 - 1974

Back Stamp	Beswick Number	Doulton Number	U.S. $	Price Can. $	U.K. £	Aust. $
BP-2	1940/1	P1940/1	600.00	750.00	300.00	800.00
BP-3a			500.00	650.00	275.00	700.00

MR. BENJAMIN BUNNY™
Second Version (Pipe In)

Modeller:	Arthur Gredington
Height:	4 1/4", 10.8 cm
Colour:	Variation No. 1 — dark maroon jacket
	Variation No. 2 — lilac jacket
Issued:	1. c.1970 - c.1974
	2. 1975 to the present

BEATRIX POTTER
"Mr. Benjamin Bunny"
© F. Warne & Co. 1965
Licensed by Copyrights
BESWICK ENGLAND

Back Stamp	Beswick Number	Colour Variation	U.S. $	Price Can. $	U.K. £	Aust. $
BP-3a	1940/2	Dark maroon	500.00	650.00	275.00	700.00
BP-3a		Lilac jacket	90.00	125.00	65.00	150.00
BP-3b		Lilac jacket	65.00	85.00	40.00	100.00
BP-3c		Lilac jacket	90.00	125.00	65.00	150.00
BP-4		Lilac jacket	95.00	110.00	50.00	125.00
BP-6		Lilac jacket	32.50	50.00	14.95	69.00

MR. BENJAMIN BUNNY AND PETER RABBIT™

Modeller:	Alan Maslankowski
Height:	4", 10.1 cm
Colour:	Benjamin Bunny — lilac jacket, yellow waistcoat
	Peter Rabbit — blue jacket
Issued:	1975 - 1995

BEATRIX POTTER'S
"Mr. Benjamin Bunny
& Peter Rabbit"
F. Warne & Co. Ltd.
© Copyright 1975
BESWICK ENGLAND

Back Stamp	Beswick Number	Doulton Number	U.S. $	Price Can. $	U.K. £	Aust. $
BP-3b	2509	P2509	175.00	225.00	85.00	250.00
BP-3c			200.00	250.00	110.00	275.00
BP-6			55.00	75.00	30.00	90.00

MR. DRAKE PUDDLE-DUCK™

Modeller:	David Lyttleton
Height:	4", 10.1 cm
Colour:	White duck, blue waistcoat and trousers
Issued:	1979 to the present

BEATRIX POTTER
"Mr. Drake Puddle-Duck"
© Frederick Warne & Co. 1979
Licensed by Copyrights
BESWICK ENGLAND

Back Stamp	Beswick Number	Doulton Number	U.S. $	Price Can. $	U.K. £	Aust. $
BP-3b	2628	P2628	65.00	100.00	45.00	100.00
BP-3c			90.00	135.00	70.00	135.00
BP-4			85.00	125.00	75.00	125.00
BP-6			32.50	50.00	14.95	69.00

MR JACKSON™
First Variation (Green Frog)

Modeller:	Albert Hallam
Height:	2 3/4", 7.0 cm
Colour:	Green frog wearing mauve jacket
Issued:	1974 - c.1974

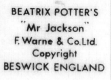

BEATRIX POTTER'S
"Mr Jackson"
F. Warne & Co. Ltd.
Copyright
BESWICK ENGLAND

Back Stamp	Beswick Number	Doulton Number	U.S. $	Price Can. $	U.K. £	Aust. $
BP-3a	2453/1	P2453/1	550.00	625.00	250.00	550.00

MR JACKSON™
Second Variation (Brown Frog)

Modeller:	Albert Hallam
Height:	2 3/4", 7.0 cm
Colour:	Brown frog wearing mauve jacket
Issued:	1975 to the present

BEATRIX POTTER'S
"Mr Jackson"
F. Warne & Co. Ltd.
© Copyright 1974
BESWICK ENGLAND

Back Stamp	Beswick Number	Doulton Number	U.S. $	Price Can. $	U.K. £	Aust. $
BP-3b	2453/2	P2453/2	85.00	130.00	65.00	140.00
BP-3c			115.00	165.00	90.00	175.00
BP-6			32.50	50.00	14.95	75.00

MR. JEREMY FISHER™
First Version, First Variation (Spotted Legs)

Modeller:	Arthur Gredington
Height:	3", 7.6 cm
Colour:	Lilac coat, green frog with small brown spots on head and legs
Issued:	1950 - c.1974

BEATRIX POTTER'S
"Mr Jeremy Fisher"
F. Warne & Co. Ltd.
Copyright
BESWICK ENGLAND

Back Stamp	Beswick Number	Doulton Number	U.S. $	Price Can. $	U.K. £	Aust. $
BP-1	1157/1	P1157/1	350.00	475.00	225.00	525.00
BP-2			300.00	350.00	160.00	375.00
BP-3a			200.00	250.00	95.00	275.00

MR. JEREMY FISHER™
First Version, Second Variation (Striped Legs)

Modeller:	Arthur Gredington
Height:	3", 7.6 cm
Colour:	Lilac coat, green frog with large spots on head and stripes on legs
Issued:	c.1950 to the present

Back Stamp	Beswick Number	Doulton Number	U.S. $	Price Can. $	U.K. £	Aust. $
BP-1	1157/2	1157/2	350.00	475.00	225.00	525.00
BP-3b			75.00	125.00	50.00	125.00
BP-3c			95.00	150.00	75.00	150.00
BP-6			32.50	50.00	14.95	69.00

MR. JEREMY FISHER™
Second Version (Large size)

Modeller:	Martyn Alcock
Height:	5", 12.7 cm
Size:	Large
Colour:	Lilac coat, green frog with stripes on legs
Issued:	1994 to the present

Back Stamp	Beswick Number	Doulton Number	U.S. $	Price Can. $	U.K. £	Aust. $
BP-7	3372	P3372	72.50	96.00	27.95	129.00

MR. JEREMY FISHER DIGGING™

Modeller:	Ted Chawner
Height:	3 3/4", 9.5 cm
Colour:	Mauve coat, pink waistcoat, white cravat, green frog with brown highlights
Issued:	1988 - 1994

Back Stamp	Beswick Number	Doulton Number	U.S. $	Price Can. $	U.K. £	Aust. $
BP-4	3090	P3090	300.00	425.00	175.00	425.00
BP-6			75.00	100.00	35.00	100.00

Note: The skin of Jeremy Fisher may have dark or light spots.

MR. McGREGOR™

Modeller:	Martyn C. R. Alcock
Height:	5 1/4", 13.5 cm
Colour:	Brown hat and trousers, tan vest and pale blue shirt
Issued:	1995 to the present

Back Stamp	Beswick Number	Doulton Number	U.S. $	Price Can. $	U.K. £	Aust. $
BP-6	3506	P3506	42.50	50.00	17.95	89.00

MR TOD™

Modeller:	Ted Chawner
Height:	4 3/4", 12.1 cm
Colour:	Green suit, red waistcoat, dark brown walking stick
Issued:	1988 - 1993

Back Stamp	Beswick Number	Doulton Number	U.S. $	Price Can. $	U.K. £	Aust. $
BP-4	3091/1	P3091/1	350.00	475.00	250.00	475.00
BP-6			95.00	135.00	40.00	125.00

Note: Variations occur with the head facing right or left and the base in either green or brown.

MRS FLOPSY BUNNY™

Modeller:	Arthur Gredington
Height:	4", 10.1 cm
Colour:	Blue dress, pink bag
Issued:	1965 to the present

Back Stamp	Beswick Number	Doulton Number	U.S. $	Price Can. $	U.K. £	Aust. $
BP-2	1942	P1942	225.00	225.00	95.00	250.00
BP-3a			150.00	175.00	90.00	175.00
BP-3b			65.00	90.00	50.00	100.00
BP-3c			90.00	130.00	70.00	130.00
BP-4			85.00	125.00	55.00	140.00
BP-6			32.50	50.00	14.95	65.00

Note: The dress is bright blue on earlier models and pale blue on later models.

MRS RABBIT™
First Version (Umbrella Out)

Modeller:	Arthur Gredington
Height:	4 1/4", 10.8 cm
Colour:	Variation No. 1 — pink and yellow striped dress
	Variation No. 2 — lilac and pale green striped dress
Issued:	1951 - c.1974

Back Stamp	Beswick Number	Variation	U.S. $	Price Can. $	U.K.£	Aust. $
BP-1	1200/1	Var. 1	550.00	625.00	300.00	600.00
BP-2		Var. 1	500.00	575.00	250.00	550.00
BP-2		Var. 2	500.00	575.00	250.00	550.00
BP-3a		Var. 2	300.00	375.00	175.00	400.00

Note: The base is too small to carry the circular Beswick England backstamp. It is flattened and the copyright date is carried in script.

MRS RABBIT™
Second Version (Umbrella Moulded to Dress)

Modeller:	Arthur Gredington
Height:	4 1/4", 10.8 cm
Colour:	Lilac and yellow striped dress, red collar and cap, light straw coloured basket
Issued:	c.1975 to the present

Back Stamp	Beswick Number	Doulton Number	U.S. $	Price Can. $	U.K. £	Aust. $
BP-3b	1200/2	P1200/2	65.00	90.00	50.00	125.00
BP-3c			95.00	125.00	75.00	150.00
BP-4			90.00	175.00	70.00	150.00
BP-6			32.50	50.00	14.95	65.00

MRS RABBIT™
Third Version (Large Size)

Modeller:	Martyn Alcock
Height:	6 1/4", 15.9 cm
Colour:	White, pink, yellow and green
Issued:	1994 to the present

Back Stamp	Beswick Number	Doulton Number	U.S. $	Price Can. $	U.K. £	Aust. $
BP-7	3398	P3398	72.50	96.00	27.95	129.00

MRS. RABBIT AND BUNNIES™

Modeller:	David Lyttleton
Height:	3 3/4", 9.5 cm
Colour:	Blue dress with white apron, dark blue chair
Issued:	1976 to the present

BEATRIX POTTER'S
Mrs. Rabbit and Bunnies
F. Warne & Co. Ltd.
© Copyright 1976
BESWICK ENGLAND

Back Stamp	Beswick Number	Doulton Number	U.S. $	Price Can. $	U.K. £	Aust. $
BP-3b	2543	P2543	85.00	125.00	45.00	135.00
BP-3c			110.00	150.00	70.00	165.00
BP-4			110.00	150.00	60.00	160.00
BP-5			135.00	165.00	95.00	185.00
BP-6			32.50	50.00	14.95	65.00

MRS RABBIT COOKING™

Modeller:	Martyn Alcock
Height:	4", 10.1 cm
Colour:	Blue dress, white apron
Issued:	1992 to the present

Back Stamp	Beswick Number	Doulton Number	U.S. $	Price Can. $	U.K. £	Aust. $
BP-6	3278	P3278	32.50	—	14.95	69.00

MRS TIGGY-WINKLE™
First Variation (Diagonal Stripes)

Modeller:	Arthur Gredington
Height:	3 1/4", 8.3 cm
Colour:	Red-brown and white dress, green and blue striped skirt, white apron
Issued:	1948 - 1974

BEATRIX POTTER'S
Mrs Tiggy-Winkle
BESWICK · ENGLAND
23
copyright

Back Stamp	Beswick Number	Doulton Number	U.S. $	Price Can.$	U.K. £	Aust. $
BP-1	1107/1	P1107/1	300.00	400.00	125.00	450.00
BP-2			275.00	350.00	100.00	400.00
BP-3a			150.00	200.00	75.00	175.00

Note: This figurine is also recognisable by the heavily patterned bustle.

MRS TIGGY-WINKLE™
Second Variation (Plaid)

Modeller:	Arthur Gredington
Height:	3 1/4", 8.3 cm
Colour:	Red-brown and white dress, green and blue striped skirt, white apron
Issued:	1972 to the present

Back Stamp	Beswick Number	Doulton Number	U.S. $	Price Can. $	U.K. £	Aust. $
BP-2	1107/2	P1107/2	275.00	350.00	100.00	400.00
BP-3b			85.00	125.00	45.00	135.00
BP-3c			110.00	150.00	70.00	165.00
BP-4			110.00	150.00	60.00	165.00
BP-6			32.50	50.00	14.95	65.00

MRS. TIGGY WINKLE TAKES TEA™

Modeller:	David Lyttleton
Height:	3 1/4", 8.3 cm
Colour:	Pink and white dress, white and brown mob cap
Issued:	1985 to the present

Back Stamp	Beswick Number	Doulton Number	U.S. $	Price Can. $	U.K. £	Aust. $
BP-3b	2877	P2877	125.00	150.00	95.00	150.00
BP-3c			150.00	175.00	110.00	175.00
BP-4			175.00	250.00	120.00	250.00
BP-6			32.50	50.00	14.95	65.00

MRS TITTLEMOUSE™

Modeller:	Arthur Gredington
Height:	3 1/2", 8.9 cm
Colour:	White and red striped blouse, blue and white striped skirt
Issued:	1948 - 1993

Back Stamp	Beswick Number	Doulton Number	U.S. $	Price Can. $	U.K. £	Aust. $
BP-1	1103	P1103	300.00	450.00	110.00	450.00
BP-2			250.00	350.00	95.00	350.00
BP-3a			90.00	125.00	80.00	135.00
BP-3b			65.00	100.00	60.00	110.00
BP-3c			90.00	125.00	80.00	135.00
BP-6			50.00	70.00	30.00	70.00

NO MORE TWIST™

Modeller:	Martyn Alcock
Height:	3 1/2", 9.2 cm
Colour:	Brown and white mouse
Issued:	1992 to the present

Back Stamp	Beswick Number	Doulton Number	U.S. $	Price Can. $	U.K. £	Aust. $
BP-6	3325	P3325	32.50	—	14.95	75.00

OLD MR. BOUNCER™

Modeller:	David Lyttleton
Height:	3", 7.6 cm
Colour:	Brown jacket and trousers, blue scarf
Issued:	1986 - 1995

Back Stamp	Beswick Number	Doulton Number	U.S. $	Price Can. $	U.K.£	Aust. $
BP-3c	2956	P2956	95.00	125.00	55.00	150.00
BP-6			45.00	60.00	25.00	70.00

OLD MR BROWN™

Modeller:	Albert Hallam
Height:	3 1/4", 8.3 cm
Colour:	Brown owl and red squirrel
Issued:	1963 to the present

Back Stamp	Beswick Number	Doulton Number	U.S. $	Price Can. $	U.K. £	Aust. $
BP-2	1796	P1796	225.00	300.00	145.00	300.00
BP-3a			90.00	125.00	70.00	125.00
BP-3b			65.00	100.00	45.00	100.00
BP-3c			90.00	125.00	70.00	125.00
BP-6			32.50	50.00	14.95	65.00

Note: The colour of the squirrel may vary from orange to brown.

BEATRIX POTTER'S
"Old Mr Pricklepin"
© Frederick Warne P.L.C. 1983
BESWICK ENGLAND

OLD MR PRICKLEPIN™

Modeller:	David Lyttleton
Height:	2 1/2", 6.4 cm
Colour:	Brown hedgehog
Issued:	1983 - 1989

Back Stamp	Beswick Number	Doulton Number	U.S. $	Price Can. $	U.K. £	Aust. $
BP-3b	2767	P2767	90.00	100.00	50.00	100.00
BP-3c			115.00	125.00	70.00	125.00
BP-6			125.00	150.00	75.00	150.00

PETER AND THE RED POCKET HANDKERCHIEF™

Modeller:	Martyn Alcock
Height:	4 3/4", 12.3 cm
Colour:	Brown blanket, light blue coat
Issued:	1991 to the present

ROYAL ALBERT ®
ENGLAND
Peter and the
Red Pocket Handkerchief
Beatrix Potter
© F. WARNE & CO. 1990
© 1990 ROYAL ALBERT LTD

Back Stamp	Beswick Number	Doulton Number	U.S. $	Price Can. $	U.K. £	Aust. $
BP-6	3242	P3242	42.50	—	15.95	75.00

PETER ATE A RADISH™

Modeller:	Warren Platt
Height:	4", 10.1 cm
Colour:	Blue jacket, brown and white rabbit, red radishes
Issued:	1995 to the present

Back Stamp	Beswick Number	Doulton Number	U.S. $	Price Can. $	U.K. £	Aust. $
BP-6	3533	P3533	42.50	57.00	16.95	74.00

PETER IN BED™

Modeller:	Martyn C. R. Alcock
Height:	2 3/4", 7.0 cm
Colour:	Blue, white, pink and green
Issued:	1995 to the present

Back Stamp	Beswick Number	Doulton Number	U.S. $	Price Can. $	U.K. £	Aust. $
BP-6	3473	P3473	42.50	69.00	18.50	85.00

PETER IN THE GOOSEBERRY NET™

Modeller:	David Lyttleton
Height:	2", 4.6 cm
Colour:	Brown and white rabbit wearing blue jacket, green netting
Issued:	1989 - 1995

ROYAL ALBERT ®
ENGLAND
Peter in the Gooseberry Net
Beatrix Potter
© F. WARNE & CO. 1989
© 1989 ROYAL ALBERT LTD

Back Stamp	Beswick Number	Doulton Number	U.S. $	Price Can. $	U.K. £	Aust. $
BP-6	3157	P3157	40.00	60.00	20.00	70.00

BEATRIX POTTER'S
Peter Rabbit
BESWICK
ENGLAND
COPYRIGHT
F. WARNE & CO. Ltd

PETER RABBIT™
First Version, First Variation (Deep Blue Jacket)

Modeller:	Arthur Gredington
Height:	4 1/2", 11.4 cm
Colour:	Brown and white rabbit wearing dark blue jacket
Issued:	1948 - c.1980

Back Stamp	Beswick Number	Doulton Number	U.S. $	Price Can. $	U.K. £	Aust. $
BP-1	1098/1	P1098/1	250.00	350.00	150.00	400.00
BP-2			225.00	275.00	125.00	325.00
BP-3a			150.00	200.00	95.00	215.00
BP-3b			125.00	175.00	75.00	185.00

Note: Peter Rabbit was issued with two different bases.

PETER RABBIT™
First Version, Second Variation
(Light Blue Jacket)

Modeller:	Arthur Gredington
Height:	4 1/2", 11.4 cm
Colour:	Brown and white rabbit wearing light blue jacket
Issued:	c.1980 to the present

BEATRIX POTTER
"Peter Rabbit"
© F. Warne & Co. 1948
Licensed by Copyrights
John Beswick
Studio of Royal Doulton
England

Back Stamp	Beswick Number	Doulton Number	U.S. $	Price Can. $	U.K. £	Aust. $
BP-3b	1098/2	P1098/2	65.00	90.00	45.00	100.00
BP-3c			90.00	120.00	65.00	130.00
BP-4			85.00	125.00	50.00	140.00
BP-5			110.00	150.00	95.00	160.00
BP-6			32.50	50.00	14.95	60.00

PETER RABBIT™
Second Version (Large Size)

Modeller:	Martyn Alcock
Height:	6 3/4", 17.1 cm
Size:	Large
Colour:	Brown rabbit wearing a blue coat
Issued:	1993 to the present

BEATRIX POTTER'S
Peter Rabbit ™
© F. WARNE & CO. 1992
© 1992 ROYAL DOULTON
1893 PETER RABBIT 1993
100
F. WARNE & CO.
BESWICK
ENGLAND

Back Stamp	Beswick Number	Doulton Number	U.S. $	Price Can. $	U.K. £	Aust. $
BP-7a	3356	P3356	72.50	96.00	27.95	125.00
BP-7b	1993 100th anniversary		95.00	125.00	50.00	140.00

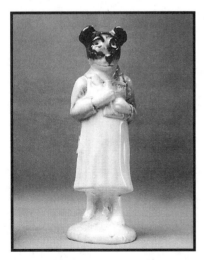

PICKLES™

Modeller:	Albert Hallam
Height:	4 1/2", 11.4 cm
Colour:	Black face dog with brown jacket and white apron, pink book
Issued:	1971 - 1982

BEATRIX POTTER'S
PICKLES
F. WARNE & CO. LTD.
COPYRIGHT
•
BESWICK 45
ENGLAND

Back Stamp	Beswick Number	Doulton Number	U.S. $	Price Can. $	U.K. £	Aust. $
BP-2	2334	P2334	750.00	1,100.00	475.00	800.00
BP-3a			475.00	625.00	300.00	675.00
BP-3b			450.00	600.00	275.00	650.00

PIGLING BLAND™
First Variation (Deep Maroon Jacket)

Modeller: Graham Orwell
Height: 4 1/4", 10.8 cm
Colour: Purple jacket, blue waistcoat, yellow trousers
Issued: 1955 - 1974

Back Stamp	Beswick Number	Doulton Number	U.S. $	Price Can. $	U.K. £	Aust. $
BP-2	1365/1	P1365/1	500.00	650.00	250.00	800.00
BP-3a			275.00	400.00	215.00	400.00
BP-3b			250.00	375.00	195.00	375.00

PIGLING BLAND™
Second Variation (Lilac Jacket)

Modeller: Graham Orwell
Height: 4 1/4", 10.8 cm
Colour: Lilac jacket, blue waistcoat, yellow trousers
Issued: c.1975 to the present

Back Stamp	Beswick Number	Doulton Number	U.S. $	Price Can. $	U.K. £	Aust. $
BP-3b	1365/2	P1365/2	65.00	100.00	50.00	110.00
BP-3c			90.00	125.00	70.00	135.00
BP-6			32.50	50.00	14.95	85.00

PIGLING EATS HIS PORRIDGE™

Modeller: Martyn Alcock
Height: 4", 10.1 cm
Colour: Brown coat, blue waistcoat and yellow trousers
Issued: 1991 - 1994

Back Stamp	Beswick Number	Doulton Number	U.S. $	Price Can. $	U.K. £	Aust. $
BP-6	3252	P3252	75.00	100.00	30.00	100.00

PIG-WIG™

Modeller: Albert Hallam
Height: 4", 10.1 cm
Colour: Variation 1 (BP-2)—grey pig, pale blue dress
Variation 2 (BP-3)—black pig, deep blue dress
Issued: 1972 - 1982

Back Stamp	Beswick Number	Doulton Number	U.S. $	Price Can. $	U.K. £	Aust. $
BP-2	2381	P2381	Extremely rare. Only two known.			
BP-3a			625.00	875.00	425.00	925.00
BP-3b			600.00	850.00	400.00	900.00

POORLY PETER RABBIT™

Modeller: David Lyttleton
Height: 3 3/4", 9.5 cm
Colour: Brown-red and white blanket
Issued: 1976 to the present

Back Stamp	Beswick Number	Doulton Number	U.S. $	Price Can. $	U.K. £	Aust. $
BP-3b	2560	P2560	75.00	100.00	50.00	125.00
BP-3c			100.00	125.00	70.00	150.00
BP-4			85.00	125.00	65.00	125.00
BP-6			32.50	50.00	14.95	60.00

Note: Later models have a lighter brown blanket.

REBECCAH PUDDLE-DUCK™

Modeller: David Lyttleton
Height: 3 1/4", 8.3 cm
Colour: White goose, pale blue coat and hat
Issued: 1981 to the present

Back Stamp	Beswick Number	Doulton Number	U.S. $	Price Can. $	U.K. £	Aust. $
BP-3b	2647	P2647	65.00	90.00	45.00	100.00
BP-3c			90.00	115.00	65.00	125.00
BP-4			85.00	125.00	55.00	140.00
BP-6			32.50	50.00	14.95	75.00

RIBBY™

Modeller:	Arthur Gredington
Height:	3 1/4", 8.3 cm
Colour:	White dress with blue rings, white apron, pink and white striped shawl
Issued:	1951 to the present

Back Stamp	Beswick Number	Doulton Number	U.S. $	Price Can. $	U.K. £	Aust. $
BP-1	1199	P1199	300.00	400.00	200.00	450.00
BP-2			225.00	300.00	150.00	325.00
BP-3a			90.00	120.00	70.00	130.00
BP-3b			65.00	95.00	50.00	100.00
BP-3c			90.00	120.00	70.00	130.00
BP-6			32.50	50.00	14.95	60.00

Note: The name shown on BP-6 is "Mrs Ribby."

RIBBY AND THE PATTY PAN™

Modeller:	Martyn Alcock
Height:	3 1/2", 8.9 cm
Colour:	Blue dress, white apron
Issued:	1992 to the present

Back Stamp	Beswick Number	Doulton Number	U.S. $	Price Can. $	U.K. £	Aust. $
BP-6	3280	P3280	32.50	—	14.95	65.00

SALLY HENNY PENNY™

Modeller:	Albert Hallam
Height:	4", 10.1 cm
Colour:	Brown and gold chicken, black hat and cloak, two yellow chicks
Issued:	1974 - 1993

Back Stamp	Beswick Number	Doulton Number	U.S. $	Price Can. $	U.K. £	Aust. $
BP-3a	2452	P2452	85.00	115.00	70.00	120.00
BP-3b			65.00	95.00	50.00	100.00
BP-3c			85.00	115.00	70.00	120.00
BP-6			50.00	60.00	30.00	75.00

Note: The confirmation of the two versions of Sally Henny Penny is still lacking. We are not able to distinguish the differences between a first and second version let alone photograph them. We have removed the versions at this time until a true distinction can be shown.

SAMUEL WHISKERS™

Modeller: Arthur Gredington
Height: 3 1/4", 8.3 cm
Colour: Light green coat, yellow
waistcoat and trousers
Issued: 1948 - 1995

Back Stamp	Beswick Number	Doulton Number	U.S. $	Price Can. $	U.K. £	Aust. $
BP-1	1106	P1106	300.00	425.00	145.00	450.00
BP-2			275.00	350.00	125.00	375.00
BP-3a			95.00	120.00	70.00	125.00
BP-3b			65.00	90.00	45.00	95.00
BP-3c			95.00	120.00	70.00	125.00
BP-4			85.00	120.00	55.00	135.00
BP-6			45.00	60.00	30.00	60.00

SIMPKIN™

Modeller: Alan Maslankowski
Height: 4", 10.1 cm
Colour: Green coat
Issued: 1975 - 1983

Back Stamp	Beswick Number	Doulton Number	U.S. $	Price Can. $	U.K. £	Aust. $
BP-3b	2508	P2508	900.00	1,200.00	525.00	900.00

SIR ISAAC NEWTON™

Modeller: Graham Tongue
Height: 3 3/4", 9.5 cm
Colour: Pale green jacket, yellow
waistcoat with tan markings
Issued: 1973 - 1984

Back Stamp	Beswick Number	Doulton Number	U.S. $	Price Can. $	U.K. £	Aust. $
BP-3a	2425	P2425	525.00	675.00	300.00	650.00
BP-3b			475.00	630.00	250.00	625.00

Note: The colour and size of Sir Isaac Newton may vary.

SQUIRREL NUTKIN™
First Variation (Red-brown Squirrel)

Modeller:	Arthur Gredington	
Height:	3 3/4", 9.5 cm	
Colour:	Red-brown squirrel holding green-brown nut	
Issued:	1948 - c.1980	

Back Stamp	Beswick Number	Doulton Number	U.S. $	Price Can. $	U.K. £	Aust. $
BP-1	1102/1	P1102/1	250.00	325.00	135.00	375.00
BP-2			225.00	275.00	110.00	300.00
BP-3a			150.00	200.00	115.00	225.00
BP-3b			125.00	175.00	95.00	250.00

SQUIRREL NUTKIN™
Second Variation (Golden Brown Squirrel)

Modeller:	Arthur Gredington	
Height:	3 3/4", 9.5 cm	
Colour:	Golden brown squirrel holding green nut	
Issued:	c.1980 to the present	

Back Stamp	Beswick Number	Doulton Number	U.S. $	Price Can. $	U.K. £	Aust. $
BP-3b	1102/2	P1102/2	65.00	95.00	45.00	100.00
BP-3c			95.00	120.00	65.00	125.00
BP-6			32.50	50.00	14.95	69.00

SUSAN™

Modeller:	David Lyttleton	
Height:	4", 10.1 cm	
Colour:	Blue dress, green, pink and black shawl and hat	
Issued:	1983 - 1989	

Back Stamp	Beswick Number	Doulton Number	U.S. $	Price Can. $	U.K. £	Aust. $
BP-3b	2716	P2716	150.00	200.00	95.00	225.00
BP-3c			175.00	225.00	115.00	250.00
BP-6			175.00	225.00	100.00	225.00

Note: The colour and size of Susan may vary.

TABITHA TWITCHIT™
First Variation (Blue Striped Top)

Modeller: Arthur Gredington
Height: 3 1/2", 8.9 cm
Colour: Blue and white striped dress, white apron
Issued: 1961 - 1974

Back Stamp	Beswick Number	Doulton Number	U.S. $	Price Can. $	U.K. £	Aust. $
BP-2	1676/1	P1676/1	350.00	400.00	150.00	400.00
BP-3a			200.00	300.00	150.00	300.00
BP-3b			175.00	275.00	125.00	275.00

TABITHA TWITCHETT™
Second Variation (White Top)

Modeller: Arthur Gredington
Height: 3 1/2", 8.9 cm
Colour: Blue and white striped dress, white apron
Issued: c.1975 - 1995

Back Stamp	Beswick Number	Doulton Number	U.S. $	Price Can. $	U.K. £	Aust. $
BP-3b	1676/2	P1676/2	65.00	90.00	45.00	100.00
BP-3c			85.00	115.00	65.00	125.00
BP-6			40.00	60.00	25.00	65.00

Note: BP-3b and forward has "Twitchett" spelled "ett."

TABITHA TWITCHIT AND MISS MOPPET™

Modeller: David Lyttleton
Height: 3 1/2", 8.9 cm
Colour: Lilac dress, white apron, yellow sponge and hassock
Issued: 1976 - 1993

Back Stamp	Beswick Number	Doulton Number	U.S. $	Price Can. $	U.K. £	Aust. $
BP-3b	2544	P2544	200.00	275.00	90.00	300.00
BP-3c			225.00	300.00	115.00	325.00
BP-4			250.00	350.00	120.00	375.00
BP-6			75.00	110.00	40.00	125.00

TAILOR OF GLOUCESTER™
First Version (Small Size)

Modeller: Arthur Gredington
Height: 3 1/2", 8.9 cm
Colour: Brown mouse, yellow
bobbin of red thread
Issued: 1949 to the present

Back Stamp	Beswick Number	Doulton Number	U.S. $	Price Can. $	U.K. £	Aust. $
BP-1	1108	P1108	300.00	450.00	200.00	475.00
BP-2			250.00	350.00	100.00	375.00
BP-3a			85.00	115.00	70.00	125.00
BP-3b			65.00	90.00	50.00	100.00
BP-3c			85.00	115.00	70.00	125.00
BP-4			85.00	125.00	50.00	135.00
BP-6			32.50	—	14.95	60.00

TAILOR OF GLOUCESTER™
Second Version (Large Size)

Modeller: Arthur Gredington
Height: 6", 15.0 cm
Colour: Brown mouse, yellow
bobbin of red thread
Issued: 1995 to the present

Back Stamp	Beswick Number	Doulton Number	U.S. $	Price Can. $	U.K. £	Aust. $
BP-7	3449	P3449	72.50	96.00	27.95	125.00

THE OLD WOMAN WHO
LIVED IN A SHOE™

Modeller: Colin Melbourne
Size: 2 3/4" x 3 3/4", 7 cm x 9.5 cm
Colour: Blue shoe
Issued: 1959 to the present

Back Stamp	Beswick Number	Doulton Number	U.S. $	Price Can. $	U.K. £	Aust. $
BP-2	1545	P1545	225.00	300.00	95.00	325.00
BP-3a			85.00	120.00	65.00	120.00
BP-3b			65.00	90.00	45.00	90.00
BP-3c			85.00	120.00	65.00	120.00
BP-6			32.50	—	14.95	90.00

THE OLD WOMAN WHO LIVED IN A SHOE KNITTING™

Modeller:	David Lyttleton
Height:	3", 7.5 cm
Colour:	Purple dress, white apron, pale blue shawl and mob cap, yellow chair
Issued:	1983 to the present

BEATRIX POTTER
"The Old Woman who lived in a Shoe.
"Knitting"
© Frederick Warne & Co. 1983
Licensed by Copyrights
BESWICK ENGLAND

Back Stamp	Beswick Number	Doulton Number	U.S. $	Price Can. $	U.K.£	Aust. $
BP-3b	2804	P2804	200.00	350.00	145.00	350.00
BP-3c			250.00	375.00	165.00	375.00
BP-6			32.50	50.00	14.95	69.00

THOMASINA TITTLEMOUSE™

Modeller:	David Lyttleton
Height:	3 1/4", 8.3 cm
Colour:	Brown and pink highlights
Issued:	1981 - 1989

BEATRIX POTTER'S
"Thomasina Tittlemouse"
F. Warne & Co Ltd.
© Copyright 1981
BESWICK ENGLAND

Correct

BEATRIX POTTER
"Tomasina Tittlemouse"
© Frederick Warne & Co. 1981
Licensed by Copyrights
BESWICK ENGLAND

Error

Backstamp Variations

Back Stamp	Beswick Number	Doulton Number	U.S. $	Price Can. $	U.K. £	Aust. $
BP-3b	2668	P2668	125.00	175.00	50.00	210.00
BP-3c	Error		150.00	200.00	70.00	240.00
BP-6			100.00	65.00	35.00	65.00

TIMMY TIPTOES™
First Variation
(Red Jacket, Brown-grey Squirrel)

Modeller:	Arthur Gredington
Height:	3 3/4", 9.5 cm
Colour:	Var. 1 — brown-grey squirrel, red jacket
	Var. 2 — grey squirrel, red jacket
Issued:	1948 - c.1980

BEATRIX POTTER'S
Timmy Tiptoes
WARNE & Co. Ltd.
COPYRIGHT
BESWICK ENGLAND

Back Stamp	Beswick Number	Doulton Number	U.S. $	Price Can. $	U.K. £	Aust. $
BP-1	1101/1	P1101/1	275.00	375.00	175.00	375.00
BP-2	Brown-grey squirrel		225.00	300.00	135.00	325.00
BP-2	Grey squirrel, red jacket		225.00	300.00	135.00	325.00
BP-3a	Brown-grey squirrel		150.00	200.00	85.00	225.00
BP-3b	Grey squirrel, red jacket		150.00	200.00	85.00	225.00

TIMMY TIPTOES™
Second Variation
(Light Pink Jacket, Grey Squirrel)

Modeller:	Arthur Gredington
Height:	3 1/2", 8.9 cm
Colour:	Grey squirrel wearing pink jacket
Issued:	c.1980 to the present

ROYAL ALBERT ®
ENGLAND
Timmy Tiptoes
Beatrix Potter
© F. WARNE & CO. 1948
© 1989 ROYAL ALBERT LTD.

Back Stamp	Beswick Number	Doulton Number	U.S. $	Price Can. $	U.K. £	Aust. $
BP-3b	1101/2	P1101/2	65.00	85.00	40.00	95.00
BP-3c			85.00	110.00	60.00	125.00
BP-6			32.50	50.00	14.95	69.00

TIMMY WILLIE FROM JOHNNY TOWN-MOUSE™

Modeller:	Arthur Gredington
Height:	2 1/2", 6.4 cm
Colour:	Brown and white mouse, green base
Issued:	1949 - 1993

BESWICK
ENGLAND
BEATRIX POTTER'S
Timmy Willie
from
Johnny Town-Mouse
copyright

Back Stamp	Beswick Number	Doulton Number	U.S. $	Price Can. $	U.K. £	Aust. $
BP-1	1109	P1109	250.00	350.00	150.00	375.00
BP-2			225.00	300.00	120.00	325.00
BP-3a			85.00	115.00	70.00	125.00
BP-3b			65.00	90.00	50.00	100.00
BP-3c			85.00	115.00	70.00	125.00
BP-4			85.00	125.00	65.00	135.00
BP-6			50.00	60.00	30.00	65.00

TIMMY WILLIE SLEEPING™

Modeller:	Graham Tongue
Size:	1 1/4" x 3 3/4", 3.2 cm x 9.5 cm
Colour:	Green, white and brown
Issued:	1986 - 1996

BEATRIX POTTER
"Timmy Willie sleeping"
© Frederick Warne & Co. 1986
Licensed by Copyrights
BESWICK ENGLAND

Back Stamp	Beswick Number	Doulton Number	U.S. $	Price Can. $	U.K. £	Aust. $
BP-3c	2996	P2996	250.00	275.00	115.00	295.00
BP-6			32.50	50.00	14.95	69.00

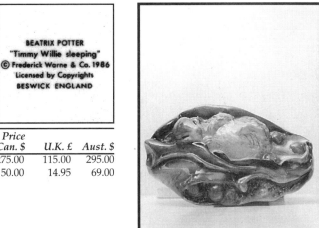

TOM KITTTEN™
First Version, First Variation
(Deep Blue Outfit)

Modeller:	Arthur Gredington
Height:	3 1/2", 8.9 cm
Colour:	Tabby kitten wearing blue trousers and jacket, dark green base
Issued:	1948 - c.1980

Back Stamp	Beswick Number	Doulton Number	U.S. $	Price Can. $	U.K. £	Aust. $
BP-1	1100/1	P1100/1	275.00	375.00	125.00	425.00
BP-2			225.00	275.00	115.00	325.00
BP-3a			90.00	125.00	70.00	125.00
BP-3b			70.00	95.00	50.00	95.00

TOM KITTEN™
First Version, Second Variation
(Light Blue Outfit)

Modeller:	Arthur Gredington
Height:	3 1/2", 8.9 cm
Colour:	Tabby kitten wearing light blue trousers and jacket, light green base
Issued:	c.1980 to the present

Back Stamp	Beswick Number	Doulton Number	U.S. $	Price Can. $	U.K. £	Aust. $
BP-3b	1100/2	P1100/2	70.00	95.00	50.00	95.00
BP-3c			90.00	115.00	70.00	115.00
BP-4			85.00	125.00	65.00	135.00
BP-6			32.50	50.00	14.95	60.00

Note: Tom Kitten was issued with two different bases.

TOM KITTEN™
Second Version (Large Size)

Modeller:	Martyn Alcock
Height:	5 1/4", 13.3 cm
Colour:	Tabby kitten wearing light blue trousers and jacket, light green base
Issued:	1994 to the present

Back Stamp	Beswick Number	Doulton Number	U.S. $	Price Can. $	U.K. £	Aust. $
BP-7	3405	P3405	72.50	96.00	27.95	129.00

TOM KITTEN AND BUTTERFLY™

Modeller:	Ted Chawner
Height:	3 1/2", 8.9 cm
Colour:	Blue outfit, yellow hat
Issued:	1987 - 1994

Back Stamp	Beswick Number	Doulton Number	U.S. $	Price Can. $	U.K. £	Aust. $
BP-3c	3030	P3030	300.00	375.00	175.00	375.00
BP-6			75.00	90.00	30.00	90.00

TOM THUMB™

Modeller:	Warren Platt
Height:	3 1/4", 8.3 cm
Colour:	Rose-pink and yellow chimney
Issued:	1987 to the present

Back Stamp	Beswick Number	Doulton Number	U.S. $	Price Can. $	U.K. £	Aust. $
BP-3c	2989	P2989	165.00	225.00	90.00	225.00
BP-6			32.50	50.00	14.95	69.00

TOMMY BROCK™
First Version, First Variation
(Handle Out, Small Eye Patch)

Modeller:	Graham Orwell
Height:	3 1/2", 8.9 cm
Colour:	Blue jacket, pink waistcoat, yellow-green trousers
Issued:	1955 - 1974

Back Stamp	Beswick Number	Doulton Number	U.S. $	Price Can. $	U.K. £	Aust. $
BP-2	1348/1	P1348/1	500.00	700.00	275.00	700.00
BP-3a			400.00	550.00	250.00	600.00

TOMMY BROCK™
First Version, Second Variation
(Handle Out, Large Eye Patch)

Modeller:	Graham Orwell
Height:	3 1/2", 8.9 cm
Colour:	Blue jacket, pink waistcoat, yellow trousers
Issued:	c.1970 - c.1974

Back Stamp	Beswick Number	Doulton Number	U.S. $	Price Can. $	U.K. £	Aust. $
BP-2	1348/2	P1348/2	500.00	700.00	275.00	700.00
BP-3a			400.00	550.00	250.00	600.00

TOMMY BROCK™
Second Version, First Variation
(Handle In, Small Eye Patch)

Modeller:	Graham Orwell
Height:	3 1/2", 8.9 cm
Colour:	Blue-grey jacket, pink waistcoat, yellow trousers
Issued:	c.1974 - 1976

Back Stamp	Beswick Number	Doulton Number	U.S. $	Price Can. $	U.K. £	Aust. $
BP-3a	1348/3	P1348/3	150.00	175.00	75.00	175.00
BP-3b			150.00	175.00	75.00	175.00

TOMMY BROCK™
Second Version, Second Variation
(Handle In, Large Eye Patch)

Modeller:	Graham Orwell
Height:	3 1/2", 8.9 cm
Colour:	Blue-grey jacket, red waistcoat, yellow trousers
Issued:	c.1975 to the present

Back Stamp	Beswick Number	Doulton Number	U.S. $	Price Can. $	U.K. £	Aust. $
BP-3b	1348/4	P1348/4	70.00	100.00	50.00	125.00
BP-3c			90.00	125.00	70.00	150.00
BP-4			85.00	125.00	60.00	135.00
BP-6			32.50	—	14.95	70.00

Note: The jacket colour varies from pale blue to dark blue in BP3b.

BEATRIX POTTER CHARACTER JUGS, PLAQUES AND MISCELLANEOUS

JEMIMA PUDDLE-DUCK CHARACTER JUG™

Modeller: Ted Chawner
Height: 4", 10.1 cm
Colour: Blue, pink and white
Issued: 1989 - 1992

BEATRIX POTTER
'Jemima Puddle-Duck'
© F. Warne & Co. 1988
Licensed by Copyrights
John Beswick
Studio of Royal Doulton
England

Back Stamp	Beswick Number	Doulton Number	U.S. $	Price Can. $	U.K. £	Aust. $
BP-4	3088	P3088	160.00	240.00	85.00	110.00
BP-6			125.00	135.00	50.00	100.00

MR. JEREMY FISHER CHARACTER JUG™

Modeller: Graham Tongue
Height: 3", 7.6 cm
Colour: Mauve
Issued: 1987 - 1992

John Beswick
ENGLAND
BEATRIX POTTER
"Jeremy Fisher"
© 1987 Frederick Warne & Co.
Licensed by Copyrights

Back Stamp	Beswick Number	Doulton Number	U.S. $	Price Can. $	U.K. £	Aust. $
BP-4	2960	P2960	140.00	175.00	75.00	150.00
BP-6			125.00	100.00	50.00	100.00

MRS. TIGGY-WINKLE CHARACTER JUG™

Modeller: Ted Chawner
Height: 3", 7.6 cm
Colour: White dress with blue stripes
Issued: 1988 - 1992

Back Stamp	Beswick Number	Doulton Number	U.S. $	Price Can. $	U.K. £	Aust.$
BP-4	3102	P3102	150.00	200.00	75.00	200.00
BP-6			115.00	150.00	60.00	150.00

OLD MR. BROWN
CHARACTER JUG™

Modeller:	Graham Tongue
Height:	3", 7.6 cm
Colour:	Brown and cream
Issued:	1987 - 1992

Back Stamp	Beswick Number	Doulton Number	U.S. $	Price Can. $	U.K.	Aust. $
BP-4	2959	P2959	160.00	215.00	80.00	215.00
BP-6			125.00	150.00	65.00	150.00

PETER RABBIT
CHARACTER JUG™

Modeller:	Graham Tongue
Height:	3", 7.6 cm
Colour:	Brown, blue and white
Issued:	1987 - 1992

Back Stamp	Beswick Number	Doulton Number	U.S. $	Price Can. $	U.K. £	Aust. $
BP-4	3006	P3006	165.00	225.00	85.00	240.00
BP-6			125.00	175.00	75.00	190.00

TOM KITTEN
CHARACTER JUG™

Modeller:	Ted Chawner
Height:	3", 7.6 cm
Colour:	Brown, blue and white
Issued:	1989 - 1992

Back Stamp	Beswick Number	Doulton Number	U.S. $	Price Can. $	U.K. £	Aust. $
BP-4	3103	P3103	165.00	225.00	85.00	100.00
BP-6			125.00	175.00	75.00	80.00

JEMIMA PUDDLE-DUCK PLAQUE™

Modeller: Albert Hallam
Height: 6", 15.2 cm
Colour: White duck, mauve shawl,
pale blue bonnet
Issued: 1967 - 1969

Back Stamp	Beswick Number	Doulton Number	U.S. $	Price Can. $	U.K. £	Aust. $
BP-2	2082	P2082		Extremely rare		

JEMIMA PUDDLE-DUCK WITH FOXY WHISKERED GENTLEMAN PLAQUE™

Modeller: Harry Sales and
David Lyttleton
Size: 7 1/2" x 7 1/2",
19.1 cm x 19.1 cm
Colour: Brown, green, white and blue
Issued: 1977 - 1982

Back Stamp	Beswick Number	Doulton Number	U.S. $	Price Can. $	U.K. £	Aust. $
BP-3	2594	P2594	150.00	175.00	75.00	235.00

MRS. TITTLEMOUSE PLAQUE™

Modeller: Harry Sales
Height: 7 1/2" x 7 1/2",
19.1 cm x 19.1 cm
Colour: Blue, pink and green
Issued: 1982 - 1984

Back Stamp	Beswick Number	Doulton Number	U.S. $	Price Can. $	U.K. £	Aust. $
BP-3	2685	P2685	150.00	200.00	95.00	150.00

PETER RABBIT PLAQUE™
First Version

Modeller:	Graham Tongue
Height:	6", 15.2 cm
Colour:	Brown rabbit wearing a blue coat
Issued:	1967 - 1969

Back Stamp	Beswick Number	Doulton Number	U.S. $	Price Can. $	U.K. £	Aust. $
BP-2	2083	P2083	Extremely rare			

Photograph not available at press time

PETER RABBIT PLAQUE™
Second Version

Modeller:	Harry Sales and David Lyttleton
Size:	7 1/2" x 7 1/2", 19.1 cm x 19.1 cm
Colour:	Blue, green, brown and orange
Issued:	1979 - 1983

Back Stamp	Beswick Number	Doulton Number	U.S. $	Price Can. $	U.K. £	Aust. $
BP-3	2650	P2650	145.00	150.00	75.00	150.00

TOM KITTEN PLAQUE™

Modeller:	Graham Tongue
Height:	6", 15.2 cm
Colour:	Unknown
Issued:	1967 - 1969

Back Stamp	Beswick Number	Doulton Number	U.S. $	Price Can. $	U.K.	Aust. $
BP-2	2085	P2085	Extremely rare			

Photograph not available at press time

DISPLAY STAND

Modeller:	Andrew Brindley
Size:	12 1/2" x 12 1/2", 31.7 cm x 31.7 cm
Colour:	Brown, light brown
Issued:	1970 to the present

Back Stamp	Beswick Number	Doulton Number	U.S. $	Price Can. $	U.K. £	Aust. $
Beswick	2295	P2295	125.00	100.00	50.00	90.00
Doulton			—	—	18.95	—

TREE LAMP BASE™

Modeller:	James Hayward and Albert Hallam
Height:	7", 17.8 cm
Colour:	Brown and green
Issued:	1958 - 1982

Back Stamp	Beswick Number	Doulton Number	U.S. $	Price Can. $	U.K. £	Aust. $
BP-2	1531	P1531	275.00	375.00	175.00	400.00
BP-3			225.00	300.00	125.00	325.00

Note: The price of this lamp will vary in accordance with the figure found on the base.

BEATRIX POTTER STUDIO SCULPTURES

SS1
TIMMY WILLIE™

Designer:	Harry Sales
Modeller:	Graham Tongue
Height:	4 1/4", 10.8 cm
Colour:	Green and brown
Issued:	1985 - 1985

Beswick Number	Price U.S. $	Can. $	U.K. £	Aust. $
SS1	100.00	150.00	65.00	130.00

SS2
FLOPSY BUNNIES™

Designer:	Harry Sales
Modeller:	Graham Tongue
Height:	5", 12.7 cm
Colour:	Browns and green
Issued:	1985 - 1985

Beswick Number	Price U.S. $	Can. $	U.K. £	Aust. $
SS2	150.00	200.00	95.00	225.00

SS3
MR. JEREMY FISHER™

Designer:	Harry Sales
Modeller:	David Lyttleton
Height:	4", 10.1 cm
Colour:	Beige and cream
Issued:	1985 - 1985

Beswick Number	Price U.S. $	Can. $	U.K. £	Aust. $
SS3	150.00	200.00	95.00	250.00

SS4
PETER RABBIT™

Designer:	Harry Sales
Modeller:	Graham Tongue
Height:	7", 17.8 cm
Colour:	Browns, blue and green
Issued:	1985 - 1985

| Beswick Number | Price | | | |
	U.S. $	Can. $	U.K. £	Aust. $
SS4	150.00	200.00	95.00	250.00

SS11
MRS. TIGGY WINKLE™

Designer:	Harry Sales
Modeller:	Graham Tongue
Height:	5", 12.7 cm
Colour:	Browns, green, white and blue
Issued:	1985 - 1985

| Beswick Number | Price | | | |
	U.S. $	Can. $	U.K. £	Aust. $
SS11	150.00	200.00	95.00	250.00

SS26
YOCK YOCK™
(In the Tub)

Designer:	Harry Sales
Modeller:	David Lyttleton
Height:	1 7/8", 5.0 cm
Colour:	Pink and brown
Issued:	1986 - 1986

| Beswick Number | Price | | | |
	U.S. $	Can. $	U.K. £	Aust. $
SS26	275.00	375.00	175.00	400.00

SS27
PETER RABBIT™
(In the Watering Can)

Designer:	Harry Sales
Modeller:	David Lyttleton
Height:	3 1/4", 8.3 cm
Colour:	Browns and blue
Issued:	1986 - 1986

Beswick Number		Price		
	U.S. $	Can. $	U.K. £	Aust. $
SS27	350.00	475.00	225.00	450.00

BEDTIME CHORUS

1801
PIANIST™

Designer:	Albert Hallam
Height:	3", 7.6 cm
Colour:	Pale blue and yellow
Issued:	1962 - 1969

Beswick		Price		
Number	U.S. $	Can. $	U.K. £	Aust. $
1801	140.00	175.00	80.00	130.00

1802
PIANO™

Designer:	Albert Hallam
Height:	3", 7.6 cm
Colour:	Brown and white
Issued:	1962 - 1969

Beswick		Price		
Number	U.S. $	Can. $	U.K. £	Aust. $
1802	125.00	150.00	50.00	130.00

1803
CAT - SINGING™

Designer:	Albert Hallam
Height:	1 1/4", 3.2 cm
Colour:	Ginger stripe
Issued:	1962 - 1971

Beswick		Price		
Number	U.S. $	Can. $	U.K. £	Aust. $
1803	85.00	110.00	55.00	130.00

1804
BOY WITHOUT SPECTACLES™

Designer:	Albert Hallam
Height:	3 1/2", 8.9 cm
Colour:	Yellow, white and blue
Issued:	1962 - 1969

Beswick		Price		
Number	U.S. $	Can. $	U.K. £	Aust. $
1804	250.00	275.00	115.00	130.00

1805
BOY WITH SPECTACLES™

Designer:	Albert Hallam
Height:	3", 7.6 cm
Colour:	Green, white and blue
Issued:	1962 - 1969

Beswick		Price		
Number	U.S. $	Can. $	U.K. £	Aust. $
1805	300.00	350.00	160.00	130.00

1824
DOG - SINGING™

Designer:	Albert Hallam
Height:	1 1/2", 3.8 cm
Colour:	Tan
Issued:	1962 - 1971

Beswick		Price		
Number	U.S. $	Can. $	U.K. £	Aust. $
1824	75.00	110.00	50.00	140.00

1825
BOY WITH GUITAR™

Designer:	Albert Hallam
Height:	3", 7.6 cm
Colour:	Blue-grey, brown and blue
Issued:	1962 - 1969

Beswick		Price		
Number	U.S. $	Can. $	U.K. £	Aust. $
1825	250.00	275.00	115.00	140.00

1826
GIRL WITH HARP™

Designer:	Albert Hallam
Height:	3 1/2", 8.9 cm
Colour:	Purple, red and brown
Issued:	1962 - 1969

Beswick		Price		
Number	U.S. $	Can. $	U.K. £	Aust. $
1826	250.00	275.00	115.00	140.00

BESWICK BEARS

BB001
WILLIAM™

Designer:	Unknown
Height:	2 1/4", 5.7 cm
Colour:	Brown bear, blue apron, white and rose book
Issued:	1993 - 1993

Beswick	Price			
Number	U.S. $	Can. $	U.K. £	Aust. $
BB001	80.00	100.00	45.00	75.00

BB002
BILLY™

Designer:	Unknown
Height:	4", 10.1 cm
Colour:	Brown bear, green waistcoat, blue hat, yellow, red and blue ball
Issued:	1993 - 1993

Beswick	Price			
Number	U.S. $	Can. $	U.K. £	Aust. $
BB002	65.00	85.00	35.00	75.00

BB003
HARRY™

Designer:	Unknown
Height:	3 1/4", 8.3 cm
Colour:	Brown bear, blue waistcoat, brown hat, white plates
Issued:	1993 - 1993

Beswick	Price			
Number	U.S. $	Can. $	U.K. £	Aust. $
BB003	65.00	85.00	35.00	75.00

BB004
BOBBY™

Designer:	Unknown
Height:	4", 10.1 cm
Colour:	Brown bear, blue waistcoat, brown hat, yellow ball, black and red bat
Issued:	1993 - 1993

Beswick Number		Price			
	U.S. $	Can. $	U.K. £	Aust. $
BB004	65.00	85.00	35.00	75.00

BB005
JAMES™

Designer:	Unknown
Height:	3 3/4", 9.5 cm
Colour:	Brown bear, yellow waistcoat, blue hat, blue parcel with pink ribbon
Issued:	1993 - 1993

Beswick Number		Price			
	U.S. $	Can. $	U.K. £	Aust. $
BB005	65.00	85.00	35.00	75.00

BB006
SUSIE™

Designer:	Unknown
Height:	3 1/2", 8.9 cm
Colour:	Brown bear, blue dress, brown recorder
Issued:	1993 - 1993

Beswick Number		Price			
	U.S. $	Can. $	U.K. £	Aust. $
BB006	65.00	85.00	35.00	75.00

BB007
ANGELA™

Designer:	Unknown
Height:	3 1/4", 8.3 cm
Colour:	Brown bear, yellow dress, white flowers
Issued:	1993 - 1993

ANGELA
kneels to pick some flowers
Happily dreaming for
hours and hours.

Beswick Bears

BB007

Beswick Number		Price		
	U.S. $	Can. $	U.K. £	Aust. $
BB007	65.00	85.00	35.00	75.00

BB008
CHARLOTTE™

Designer:	Unknown
Height:	4", 10.1 cm
Colour:	Brown bear, pink dress, blue and yellow parasol
Issued:	1993 - 1993

CHARLOTTE
tries to keep in the shade.
Twirling her parasol,
a pretty young maid.

Beswick Bears

BB008

Beswick Number		Price		
	U.S. $	Can. $	U.K. £	Aust. $
BB008	65.00	85.00	35.00	75.00

BB009
SAM™

Designer:	Unknown
Height:	3 1/2", 8.9 cm
Colour:	Brown bear, rose waistcoat, yellow banjo
Issued:	1993 - 1993

SAM
plays his banjo all day long.
Amusing friends
with a tune and a song.

Beswick Bears

BB009

Beswick Number		Price		
	U.S. $	Can. $	U.K. £	Aust. $
BB009	65.00	85.00	35.00	75.00

BB010
LIZZY™

Designer:	Unknown
Height:	2 1/4", 5.7 cm
Colour:	Brown bear, pink dress, paint box
Issued:	1993 - 1993

Beswick Number	U.S. $	Can. $	*Price* U.K. £	Aust. $
BB010	65.00	85.00	35.00	75.00

BB011
EMILY™

Designer:	Unknown
Height:	3 1/2", 8.9 cm
Colour:	Brown bear, pale blue dress, brown picnic hamper
Issued:	1993 - 1993

Beswick Number	U.S. $	Can. $	*Price* U.K. £	Aust. $
BB011	65.00	85.00	35.00	75.00

BB012
SARAH™

Designer:	Unknown
Height:	3 1/4", 8.3 cm
Colour:	Brown bear, green dress, white cup and saucer
Issued:	1993 - 1993

Beswick Number	U.S. $	Can. $	*Price* U.K. £	Aust. $
BB012	65.00	85.00	35.00	75.00

BRAMBLY HEDGE

DBH1
POPPY EYEBRIGHT™

Designer:	Harry Sales
Modeller:	David Lyttleton
Height:	3 1/4", 9.5 cm
Colour:	Grey-white and pink dress, white apron trimmed with blue flowers
Issued:	1982 to the present

Back Stamp		Price		
	U.S. $	*Can. $*	*U.K. £*	*Aust. $*
BH-1	45.00	58.00	16.95	69.00

DBH2
MR APPLE™

Designer:	Harry Sales
Modeller:	David Lyttleton
Height:	3 1/4", 8.3 cm
Colour:	Black trousers, white and blue striped shirt, white apron
Issued:	1982 to the present

Back Stamp		Price		
	U.S. $	*Can. $*	*U.K. £*	*Aust. $*
BH-1	45.00	58.00	16.95	69.00

DBH3
MRS. APPLE™

Designer:	Harry Sales
Modeller:	David Lyttleton
Height:	3 1/4", 8.3 cm
Colour:	White and blue striped dress, white apron
Issued:	1982 to the present

Back Stamp		Price		
	U.S. $	*Can. $*	*U.K. £*	*Aust. $*
BH-1	45.00	58.00	16.95	65.00

DBH4
LORD WOODMOUSE™

Designer:	Harry Sales
Modeller:	David Lyttleton
Height:	3 1/4", 8.3 cm
Colour:	Green trousers, brown coat and burgundy waistcoat
Issued:	1982 to the present

Back Stamp		Price			
	U.S. $	Can. $	U.K. £	Aust. $
BH-1	45.00	58.00	16.95	69.00

DBH5
LADY WOODMOUSE™

Designer:	Harry Sales
Modeller:	David Lyttleton
Height:	3 1/4", 8.3 cm
Colour:	Red and white striped dress, white apron
Issued:	1982 to the present

Back Stamp		Price			
	U.S. $	Can. $	U.K. £	Aust. $
BH-1	45.00	58.00	16.95	69.00

DBH6
DUSTY DOGWOOD™

Designer:	Harry Sales
Modeller:	David Lyttleton
Height:	3 1/4", 8.3 cm
Colour:	Dark grey suit, red waistcoat
Issued:	1982 to the present

Back Stamp		Price			
	U.S. $	Can. $	U.K. £	Aust. $
BH-1	45.00	58.00	16.95	69.00

DBH7
WILFRED TOADFLAX™

Designer:	Harry Sales
Modeller:	David Lyttleton
Height:	3 1/4", 8.3 cm
Colour:	Grey trousers, red and white striped shirt
Issued:	1982 to the present

Back Stamp	Price			
	U.S. $	Can. $	U.K. £	Aust. $
BH-1	45.00	58.00	16.95	64.00

DBH8
PRIMROSE WOODMOUSE™

Designer:	Harry Sales
Modeller:	David Lyttleton
Height:	3 1/4", 8.3 cm
Colour:	Yellow dress with white apron
Issued:	1982 to the present

Back Stamp	Price			
	U.S. $	Can. $	U.K. £	Aust. $
BH-1	45.00	58.00	16.95	65.00

DBH9
OLD MRS EYEBRIGHT™

Designer:	Harry Sales
Modeller:	David Lyttleton
Height:	3 1/4", 8.3 cm
Colour:	Mauve skirt, white and pink striped shawl, white apron
Issued:	1983 - 1996

Back Stamp	Price			
	U.S. $	Can. $	U.K. £	Aust. $
BH-1	45.00	58.00	25.00	64.00

DBH10
MR. TOADFLAX™

Designer:	Harry Sales
Modeller:	David Lyttleton
Height:	3 1/4", 8.3 cm
Colour:	Blue and white striped shirt, pink trousers
Issued:	1983 to the present

Back Stamp		Price		
	U.S. $	Can. $	U.K. £	Aust. $
BH-1	45.00	58.00	16.95	64.00

DBH11
MRS. TOADFLAX™

Designer:	Harry Sales
Modeller:	David Lyttleton
Height:	3 1/4", 8.3 cm
Colour:	Green and white striped dress, white apron
Issued:	1985 - 1996

Back Stamp		Price		
	U.S. $	Can. $	U.K. £	Aust. $
BH-1	45.00	58.00	25.00	64.00

DBH12
CATKIN™

Designer:	Harry Sales
Modeller:	David Lyttleton
Height:	3 1/4", 8.3 cm
Colour:	Yellow dress with white apron
Issued:	1985 - 1994

Back Stamp		Price		
	U.S. $	Can. $	U.K. £	Aust. $
BH-1	55.00	75.00	35.00	64.00

DBH13
OLD VOLE™

Designer:	Harry Sales
Modeller:	David Lyttleton
Height:	3 1/4", 8.3 cm
Colour:	Green jacket, blue trousers, yellow waistcoat
Issued:	1985 - 1992

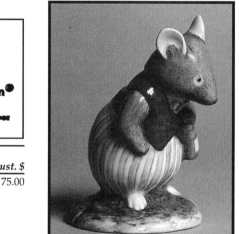

Back Stamp	Price			
	U.S. $	Can. $	U.K. £	Aust. $
BH-1	110.00	175.00	60.00	75.00

DBH14
BASIL™

Designer:	Harry Sales
Modeller:	David Lyttleton
Height:	3 1/4", 8.3 cm
Colour:	Brown waistcoat, green and white striped trousers
Issued:	1985 - 1992

Back Stamp	Price			
	U.S. $	Can. $	U.K. £	Aust. $
BH-1	100.00	140.00	60.00	75.00

DBH15
MRS. CRUSTYBREAD™

Designer:	Graham Tongue
Modeller:	Ted Chawner
Height:	3 1/4", 8.3 cm
Colour:	Yellow dress, white apron and cap
Issued:	1987 - 1994

Back Stamp	Price			
	U.S. $	Can. $	U.K. £	Aust. $
BH-1	45.00	60.00	35.00	64.00

DBH16
CLOVER™

Designer:	Graham Tongue
Modeller:	Graham Tongue
Height:	3 1/4", 8.3 cm
Colour:	Burgundy dress, white apron
Issued:	1987 to the present

Royal Doulton®
CLOVER
D B H 16
FROM THE BRAMBLY HEDGE
GIFT COLLECTION
© 1987 JILL BARKLEM

Back Stamp	Price			
	U.S. $	Can. $	U.K. £	Aust. $
BH-1	45.00	58.00	16.95	59.00

DBH17
TEASEL™

Designer:	Graham Tongue
Modeller:	Ted Chawner
Height:	3 1/4", 8.3 cm
Colour:	Blue-grey dungarees, blue and white striped shirt
Issued:	1987 - 1993

Royal Doulton®
TEASEL
D B H 17
FROM THE BRAMBLY HEDGE
GIFT COLLECTION
© 1987 JILL BARKLEM

Back Stamp	Price			
	U.S. $	Can. $	U.K. £	Aust. $
BH-1	115.00	150.00	60.00	75.00

DBH18
STORE STUMP MONEY BOX™

Designer:	Martyn Alcock
Height:	3 1/4", 8.3 cm
Colour:	Brown
Issued:	1987 - 1996

Royal Doulton®
STORE STUMP MONEY BOX
D B H 18
FROM THE BRAMBLY HEDGE
GIFT COLLECTION
© 1987 JILL BARKLEM

Back Stamp	Price			
	U.S. $	Can. $	U.K. £	Aust. $
BH-1	80.00	95.00	50.00	75.00

DBH19
LILY WEAVER™

Designer:	Graham Tongue
Modeller:	Ted Chawner
Height:	3 1/4", 8.3 cm
Colour:	White dress with green and mauve, white cap
Issued:	1988 - 1993

Back Stamp	Price			
	U.S. $	Can. $	U.K. £	Aust. $
BH-1	75.00	135.00	45.00	75.00

DBH20
FLAX WEAVER™

Designer:	Graham Tongue
Modeller:	Ted Chawner
Height:	3 1/4", 8.3 cm
Colour:	Grey trousers, grey and white striped shirt
Issued:	1988 - 1993

Back Stamp	Price			
	U.S. $	Can. $	U.K. £	Aust. $
BH-1	75.00	135.00	45.00	75.00

DBH21
CONKER™

Designer:	Graham Tongue
Modeller:	Ted Chawner
Height:	3 1/4", 8.3 cm
Colour:	Green jacket, yellow waistcoat, green striped trousers
Issued:	1988 - 1994

Back Stamp	Price			
	U.S. $	Can. $	U.K. £	Aust. $
BH-1	55.00	75.00	35.00	64.00

DBH22
PRIMROSE ENTERTAINS™

Designer: Graham Tongue
Modeller: Alan Maslankowski
Height: 3 1/4", 8.3 cm
Colour: Green and yellow dress
Issued: 1991 - 1996

Back Stamp	Price			
	U.S. $	Can. $	U.K. £	Aust. $
BH-1	65.00	100.00	30.00	110.00

DBH23
WILFRED ENTERTAINS™

Designer: Graham Tongue
Modeller: Alan Maslankowski
Height: 3 1/4", 8.3 cm
Colour: Burgundy and yellow outfit, black hat
Issued: 1991 - 1996

Back Stamp	Price			
	U.S. $	Can. $	U.K. £	Aust $
BH-1	65.00	100.00	30.00	110.00

DBH24
MR. SALTAPPLE™

Designer: Graham Tongue
Modeller: Warren Platt
Height: 3 1/4", 8.3 cm
Colour: Blue and white striped outfit, beige base
Issued: 1993 to the present

Back Stamp	Price			
	U.S. $	Can. $	U.K. £	Aust. $
BH-1	45.00	58.00	16.95	79.00

DBH25
MRS. SALTAPPLE™

Designer:	Graham Tongue
Modeller:	Warren Platt
Height:	3 1/4", 8.3 cm
Colour:	Rose and cream dress, beige hat and base
Issued:	1993 to the present

Royal Doulton®
MRS. SALTAPPLE
DBH 25
FROM THE BRAMBLY HEDGE
GIFT COLLECTION
© JILL BARKLEM 1992

Back		Price		
Stamp	U.S. $	Can. $	U.K. £	Aust. $
BH-1	45.00	58.00	16.95	79.00

DBH26
DUSTY AND BABY™

Designer:	Graham Tongue
Modeller:	Martyn C. R. Alcock
Height:	3 3/4", 9.5 cm
Colour:	Dusty - blue striped shirt with beige dungarees Baby - white gown
Issued:	1995 to the present

Back		Price		
Stamp	U.S. $	Can. $	U.K. £	Aust. $
BH-1	45.00	58.00	16.95	69.00

BUNNYKINS

BUNNYKINS BACKSTAMPS

BK-1. DOULTON & CO. LIMITED, 1972 - 1976

These backstamps were used on all figurines introduced between 1972 and 1976.

BK-2. ROYAL DOULTON TABLEWARE LTD, 1976 - 1984

The name "Doulton & Co. Limited" was changed to "Royal Doulton Tableware Ltd.," and this backstamp was used on all new figurines introduced between 1976 and 1984. It was also used on all models that had been in production previously, updating the older backstamp (BK-1). In these instances the copyright year on the stamps was kept the same as that of the original backstamp (BK-1).

BK-3. GOLDEN JUBILEE CELEBRATION, 1984

All models manufactured during 1984 carried the words "Golden Jubilee Celebration 1984," which were added to the 1976-1984 backstamp (BK-2).

BK-4. ROYAL DOULTON (U.K.), 1985 - 1986

The backstamp of 1976-1984 was modified to "Royal Doulton (U.K.)." All items introduced between 1985 and 1986 carry this backstamp.

BK-5. ROYAL DOULTON, 1987 TO DATE

BK-SPECIALS. SPECIAL COMMISSION BACKSTAMPS

The backstamp of 1985 - 1986 was again modified by removing the "(U.K.)." All new figurines introduced since 1987 carry this backstamp.

Many figurines are issued for special events, anniversaries, promotions, etc. All these carry a special stamp.

D6003

D6004

D6002

D6025

D6001

D6024

BILLY BUNNYKINS™
D6001

Designer:	Charles Noke
Height:	4 1/2", 11.4 cm
Colour:	Brown bunny, red trousers blue jacket, white bowtie with blue spots
Issued:	1939-c.1940

FARMER BUNNYKINS™
D6003

Designer:	Charles Noke
Height:	7 1/2", 19 cm
Colour:	Green, blue, brown, red and white
Issued:	1939-c.1940

FREDDIE BUNNYKINS™
D6024

Designer:	Charles Noke
Height:	3 3/4", 9.5 cm
Colour:	Brown bunny, green trousers red jacket and yellow bowtie
Issued:	1939-c.1940

MARY BUNNYKINS™
D6002

Designer:	Charles Noke
Height:	6 1/2", 16.5 cm
Colour:	Brown bunny, blue and red dress with white apron
Issued:	1939-c.1940

MOTHER BUNNYKINS™
D6004

Designer:	Charles Noke
Height:	7", 17.5 cm
Colour:	Blue, red, white and brown
Issued:	1939-c.1940

REGGIE BUNNYKINS™
D6025

Designer:	Charles Noke
Height:	3 3/4", 9.5 cm
Colour:	Brown bunny, blue dress and red bowtie
Issued:	1939-c.1940

Name	Back Stamp	Doulton Number	Price U.S. $	Can. $	U.K. £	Aust. $
Billy Bunnykins	BK-	D6001	3,200.00	3,500.00	2,000.00	3,000.00
Farmer Bunnykins	BK-	D6003	3,500.00	3,700.00	2,000.00	3,000.00
Freddie Bunnykins	BK-	D6024	4,000.00	4,250.00	2,250.00	3,000.00
Mary Bunnykins	BK-	D6002	3,500.00	3,700.00	2,000.00	3,000.00
Mother Bunnykins	BK-	D6004	3,500.00	3,700.00	2,000.00	3,000.00
Reggie Bunnykins	BK-	D6025	4,000.00	4,250.00	2,250.00	3,000.00

D6615A
BUNNYBANK™
First Variation

Designer:	Unknown
Modeller:	Unknown
Height:	8 1/2", 21.6 cm
Colour:	Grey rabbit, green coat and hat, maroon drum
Issued:	1967 - 1977

Back Stamp		Price		
	U.S. $	Can. $	U.K. £	Aust. $
BK-	350.00	375.00	200.00	450.00

D6615B
BUNNYBANK™
Second Variation

Designer:	Unknown
Modeller:	Unknown
Height:	9 1/4", 23.5 cm
Colour:	Brown rabbit, green coat and hat, maroon drum
Issued:	1979 - 1991

Back Stamp		Price		
	U.S. $	Can. $	U.K. £	Aust. $
BK-	250.00	275.00	175.00	450.00

Bunnybank
D.6615
© DOULTON & CO.LIMITED 1967

DB1
FAMILY PHOTOGRAPH BUNNYKINS ™
First Variation

Designer:	Walter Hayward
Modeller:	Albert Hallam
Height:	4 1/2", 11.4 cm
Colour:	Blue, white, burgundy and grey
Issued:	1972 - 1988 (© 1972)
Varieties:	DB67; also called "Father, Mother and Victoria Bunnykins," DB68

Back Stamp	Price U.S. $	Can. $	U.K. £	Aust. $
BK-1	125.00	175.00	75.00	225.00
BK-2	125.00	175.00	75.00	225.00
BK-3	150.00	200.00	100.00	250.00

DB2
BUNTIE BUNNYKINS HELPING MOTHER™

Designer:	Walter Hayward
Modeller:	Albert Hallam
Height:	3 1/2", 8.9 cm
Colour:	Rose-pink and yellow
Issued:	1972 - 1993 (© 1972)

Back Stamp	Price U.S. $	Can. $	U.K. £	Aust. $
BK-1	60.00	90.00	30.00	85.00
BK-2	60.00	90.00	30.00	85.00
BK-3	100.00	150.00	65.00	100.00

DB3
BILLIE BUNNYKINS COOLING OFF™

Designer:	Walter Hayward
Modeller:	Albert Hallam
Height:	3 3/4", 9.5 cm
Colour:	Burgundy, yellow and green-grey
Issued:	1972 - 1987 (© 1972)

Back Stamp	Price U.S. $	Can. $	U.K. £	Aust. $
BK-1	200.00	275.00	150.00	225.00
BK-2	200.00	275.00	150.00	225.00
BK-3	225.00	300.00	175.00	250.00

DB4
BILLIE AND BUNTIE BUNNYKINS
SLEIGH RIDE™
First Variation

Designer:	Walter Hayward
Modeller:	Albert Hallam
Height:	3 1/4", 8.3 cm
Colour:	Blue, maroon and yellow
Issued:	1972 to the present (© 1972)
Varieties:	DB81

Back Stamp	U.S. $	Can. $	U.K. £	Aust. $
BK-1	40.00	49.00	15.00	64.00
BK-2	40.00	49.00	14.95	64.00
BK-3	100.00	125.00	60.00	100.00

(Price)

DB5
MR. BUNNYKINS AUTUMN DAYS™

Designer:	Walter Hayward
Modeller:	Albert Hallam
Height:	4', 10.1 cm
Colour:	Maroon, yellow and blue
Issued:	1972 - 1982 (© 1972)

Back Stamp	U.S. $	Can. $	U.K. £	Aust. $
BK-1	400.00	450.00	225.00	800.00
BK-2	400.00	450.00	225.00	800.00
BK-3	450.00	500.00	250.00	850.00

(Price)

DB6
MRS. BUNNYKINS CLEAN SWEEP™

Designer:	Walter Hayward
Modeller:	Albert Hallam
Height:	4", 10.1 cm
Colour:	Blue and white
Issued:	1972 - 1991(© 1972)

Back Stamp	U.S. $	Can. $	U.K. £	Aust. $
BK-1	75.00	95.00	45.00	70.00
BK-2	75.00	95.00	45.00	70.00
BK-3	100.00	150.00	75.00	100.00

(Price)

DB7
DAISIE BUNNYKINS SPRING TIME™

Designer:	Walter Hayward
Modeller:	Albert Hallam
Height:	3 1/2", 8.9 cm
Colour:	Blue, white and yellow
Issued:	1972 - 1983 (© 1972)

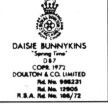

Back		Price		
Stamp	U.S. $	Can. $	U.K. £	Aust. $
BK-1	475.00	525.00	275.00	1,000.00
BK-2	475.00	525.00	275.00	1,000.00
BK-3	500.00	575.00	300.00	1,000.00

DB8
DOLLIE BUNNYKINS PLAYTIME™
First Variation

Designer:	Walter Hayward
Modeller:	Albert Hallam
Height:	4", 10.1 cm
Colour:	White dress with pink design, blue dress
Issued:	1972 - 1993 (© 1972)
Varieties:	DB80

Back		Price		
Stamp	U.S. $	Can. $	U.K. £	Aust. $
BK-1	60.00	75.00	30.00	70.00
BK-2	60.00	75.00	30.00	70.00
BK-3	85.00	125.00	65.00	100.00

DB9
STORYTIME BUNNYKINS™
First Variation

Designer:	Walter Hayward
Modeller:	Albert Hallam
Height:	3", 7.6 cm
Colour:	White dress with blue design, pink dress
Issued:	1972 to the present (© 1972)
Varieties:	DB59; also called "Partners in Collecting," DB151

Back		Price		
Stamp	U.S. $	Can. $	U.K. £	Aust. $
BK-1	40.00	49.00	35.00	70.00
BK-2	40.00	49.00	14.95	70.00
BK-3	75.00	100.00	60.00	100.00

DB10
BUSY NEEDLES BUNNYKINS™

Designer:	Walter Hayward
Modeller:	Albert Hallam
Height:	3 1/4", 8.3 cm
Colour:	White, green and maroon
Issued:	1973 - 1988 (©1974)
Varieties:	DB70

Back Stamp	Price			
	U.S. $	Can. $	U.K. £	Aust. $
BK-1	100.00	140.00	70.00	250.00
BK-2	100.00	140.00	70.00	250.00
BK-3	130.00	175.00	95.00	275.00

DB11
RISE AND SHINE BUNNYKINS™

Designer:	Walter Hayward
Modeller:	Albert Hallam
Height:	3 3/4", 9.5 cm
Colour:	Maroon, yellow and blue
Issued:	1973 - 1988 (© 1974)

Back Stamp	Price			
	U.S. $	Can. $	U.K. £	Aust. $
BK-1	140.00	175.00	95.00	250.00
BK-2	140.00	175.00	95.00	250.00
BK-3	175.00	225.00	125.00	275.00

DB12
TALLY HO! BUNNYKINS ™
First Variation

Designer:	Walter Hayward
Modeller:	Albert Hallam
Height:	3 3/4", 9.5 cm
Colour:	Burgundy, yellow, blue, white and green
Issued:	1973 - 1988 (© 1974)
Varieties:	DB78; also called "William Bunnykins," DB69

Back Stamp	Price			
	U.S. $	Can. $	U.K. £	Aust. $
BK-1	90.00	150.00	40.00	250.00
BK-2	90.00	150.00	40.00	250.00
BK-3	115.00	175.00	75.00	275.00

DB13
THE ARTIST BUNNYKINS™

Designer:	Walter Hayward
Modeller:	Alan Maslankowski
Height:	3 3/4", 9.5 cm
Colour:	Burgundy, yellow and blue
Issued:	1974 - 1982 (© 1975)

Back Stamp	Price			
	U.S. $	Can. $	U.K. £	Aust. $
BK-1	425.00	550.00	300.00	650.00
BK-2	425.00	550.00	300.00	650.00

DB14
GRANDPA'S STORY BUNNYKINS™

Designer:	Walter Hayward
Modeller:	Alan Maslankowski
Height:	4", 10.1 cm
Colour:	Burgundy, grey, yellow, blue and green
Issued:	1974 - 1983 (© 1975)

Back Stamp	Price			
	U.S. $	Can. $	U.K. £	Aust. $
BK-1	425.00	600.00	300.00	850.00
BK-2	425.00	600.00	300.00	850.00

DB15
SLEEPYTIME BUNNYKINS™

Designer:	Walter Hayward
Modeller:	Alan Maslankowski
Height:	1 3/4", 4.7 cm
Colour:	Brown, white, yellow, blue and red
Issued:	1974 - 1993 (© 1975)

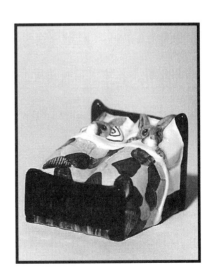

Back Stamp	Price			
	U.S. $	Can. $	U.K. £	Aust. $
BK-1	85.00	100.00	35.00	75.00
BK-2	85.00	100.00	35.00	75.00
BK-3	115.00	130.00	75.00	100.00

DB16
MR. BUNNYBEAT STRUMMING™

Designer:	Harry Sales
Modeller:	David Lyttleton
Height:	4 1/2", 11.4 cm
Colour:	Pink and yellow coat, blue and white striped trousers, white with blue polka-dot neck bow
Issued:	1982 - 1988 (© 1981)

MR. BUNNYBEAT
"Strumming"
DB 16
© ROYAL DOULTON
TABLEWARE LTD. 198

Back Stamp	Price			
	U.S. $	Can. $	U.K. £	Aust. $
BK-2	175.00	200.00	90.00	250.00
BK-3	200.00	225.00	115.00	275.00

DB17
SANTA BUNNYKINS HAPPY CHRISTMAS™

Designer:	Harry Sales
Modeller:	David Lyttleton
Height:	4 1/2", 10.8 cm
Colour:	Red, white and brown
Issued:	1981 to the present (© 1981)

SANTA BUNNYKINS
"Happy Christmas"
DB 17
© ROYAL DOULTON
TABLEWARE LTD. 1981

Back Stamp	Price			
	U.S. $	Can. $	U.K. £	Aust. $
BK-2	40.00	55.00	17.95	70.00
BK-3	60.00	75.00	60.00	100.00

DB18
MR BUNNYKINS AT THE EASTER PARADE™
First Variation

Designer:	Harry Sales
Modeller:	David Lyttleton
Height:	5", 12.7 cm
Colour:	Red, yellow and brown
Issued:	1982 - 1993 (© 1982)
Varieties:	DB 51

MR BUNNYKINS
"At The Easter Parade"
DB 18
© ROYAL DOULTON
TABLEWARE LTD. 1982

Back Stamp	Price			
	U.S. $	Can. $	U.K. £	Aust. $
BK-2	75.00	95.00	30.00	95.00
BK-3	100.00	125.00	60.00	125.00

DB19
MRS BUNNYKINS
AT THE EASTER PARADE ™
First Variation

Designer:	Harry Sales
Modeller:	David Lyttleton
Height:	4 1/2", 11.4 cm
Colour:	Pale blue and maroon
Issued:	1982 to the present (© 1982)
Varieties:	DB52

Back Stamp	Price U.S. $	Can. $	U.K. £	Aust. $
BK-2	40.00	85.00	17.95	95.00
BK-3	65.00	85.00	60.00	125.00

DB20
ASTRO BUNNYKINS ROCKET MAN™

Designer:	Harry Sales
Modeller:	David Lyttleton
Height:	4 1/4", 10.8 cm
Colour:	White, red, blue and yellow
Issued:	1983 - 1988 (© 1982)

Back Stamp	Price U.S. $	Can. $	U.K. £	Aust. $
BK-2	125.00	140.00	60.00	135.00
BK-3	150.00	175.00	95.00	160.00

DB21
HAPPY BIRTHDAY BUNNYKINS™

Designer:	Harry Sales
Modeller:	Graham Tongue
Height:	3 3/4", 9.5 cm
Colour:	Red and blue
Issued:	1983 to the present (© 1982)

Back Stamp	Price U.S. $	Can. $	U.K. £	Aust. $
BK-2	40.00	59.50	17.95	65.00
BK-3	65.00	85.00	60.00	90.00

DB22
JOGGING BUNNYKINS™

Designer:	Harry Sales
Modeller:	David Lyttleton
Height:	2 1/2", 6.4 cm
Colour:	Yellow, blue and white
Issued:	1983 - 1989 (© 1982)

Back Stamp	Price			
	U.S. $	Can. $	U.K. £	Aust. $
BK-2	100.00	120.00	55.00	135.00
BK-3	125.00	150.00	85.00	160.00

DB23
SOUSAPHONE BUNNYKINS ™
First Variation

Designer:	Harry Sales
Modeller:	David Lyttleton
Height:	3 1/2", 8.9 cm
Colour:	Red, blue and yellow
Issued:	1984 - 1990 (© 1983)
Varieties:	DB86, DB105
Series:	Bunnykins Oompah Band

Back Stamp	Price			
	U.S. $	Can. $	U.K. £	Aust. $
BK-3	130.00	175.00	75.00	175.00
BK-4	100.00	135.00	50.00	150.00

DB24
TRUMPETER BUNNYKINS™
First Variation

Designer:	Harry Sales
Modeller:	David Lyttleton
Height:	3 1/2", 8.9 cm
Colour:	Red, blue and yellow
Issued:	1984 - 1990
Varieties:	DB87, DB106
Series:	Bunnykins Oompah Band

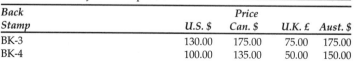

Back Stamp	Price			
	U.S. $	Can. $	U.K. £	Aust. $
BK-3	130.00	175.00	75.00	175.00
BK-4	100.00	135.00	50.00	150.00

DB25
CYMBALS BUNNYKINS™
First Variation

Designer:	Harry Sales
Modeller:	David Lyttleton
Height:	3 1/2", 8.9 cm
Colour:	Red, blue and yellow
Issued:	1984 - 1990 (© 1972)
Varieties:	DB 88, DB 107
Series:	Bunnykins Oompah Band

Back	Price			
Stamp	U.S. $	Can. $	U.K. £	Aust. $
BK-3	130.00	175.00	75.00	175.00
BK-4	100.00	135.00	50.00	150.00

DB26A
DRUMMER BUNNYKINS™
50th Anniversary Edition
First Variation

Designer:	Harry Sales
Modeller:	David Lyttleton
Height:	3 1/2", 9.2 cm
Colour:	Blue, yellow, red and cream
Issued:	1984 - 1984
Series:	Bunnykins Oompah Band

Back	Price			
Stamp	U.S. $	Can. $	U.K. £	Aust. $
BK-3	125.00	175.00	100.00	175.00

DB26B
DRUMMER BUNNYKINS ™
Bunnykins Oompah Band Edition
Second Variation

Designer:	Harry Sales
Modeller:	David Lyttleton
Height:	3 3/4", 9.5 cm
Colour:	Blue, yellow, red and cream
Issued:	1984 - 1990 (© 1983)
Varieties:	DB 89, DB 108
Series:	Bunnykins Oompah Band

Back	Price			
Stamp	U.S. $	Can. $	U.K £	Aust. $
BK-4	100.00	150.00	65.00	150.00

DB27
DRUM-MAJOR BUNNYKINS™
First Variation

Designer:	Harry Sales
Modeller:	David Lyttleton
Height:	3 1/2", 8.9 cm
Colour:	Red, blue and yellow
Issued:	1984 - 1990
Varieties:	DB 90, DB 109
Series:	Bunnykins Oompah Band

Back Stamp	Price			
	U.S. $	Can. $	U.K. £	Aust. $
BK-3	130.00	175.00	75.00	175.00
BK-4	100.00	135.00	50.00	150.00

DB28A
OLYMPIC BUNNYKINS™
First Variation

Designer:	Harry Sales
Modeller:	David Lyttleton
Height:	3 3/4", 9.4 cm
Colour:	White and blue
Issued:	1984 - 1988

Back Stamp	Price			
	U.S. $	Can. $	U.K. £	Aust. $
BK-3	175.00	250.00	100.00	150.00
BK-4	150.00	225.00	85.00	125.00

DB28B
OLYMPIC BUNNYKINS ™
Second Variation

Designer:	Harry Sales
Modeller:	David Lyttleton
Height:	3 1/2", 8.9 cm
Colour:	Gold and green
Issued:	1984 - 1984 (© 1983)

Back Stamp	Price			
	U.S. $	Can. $	U.K. £	Aust. $
BK-Special	250.00	275.00	135.00	450.00

Note: Made exclusively for the Australian market.

DB29A
TOUCHDOWN BUNNYKINS ™
First Variation

Designer:	Harry Sales
Modeller:	David Lyttleton
Height:	3 1/4", 8.3 cm
Colour:	Blue and white
Issued:	1985 - 1988
Varieties:	DB 96, DB 100

"TOUCHDOWN BUNNYKINS"
DB 29
© ROYAL DOULTON
TABLEWARE LTD 1984
GOLDEN JUBILEE
CELEBRATION 1984

Back Stamp	Price			
	U.S. $	Can. $	U.K. £	Aust. $
BK-4	95.00	165.00	65.00	300.00
BK-5	95.00	165.00	65.00	300.00

DB29B
TOUCHDOWN BUNNYKINS™
Second Variation (Boston College)

Designer:	Harry Sales
Modeller:	David Lyttleton
Height:	3 1/4", 8.3 cm
Colour:	Maroon and gold
Issued:	1985 in a limited edition of 50

Back Stamp	Price			
	U.S. $	Can. $	U.K. £	Aust. $
BK-Special	2,200.00	2,000.00	800.00	1,750.00

DB30
KNOCKOUT BUNNYKINS™

Designer:	Harry Sales
Modeller:	David Lyttleton
Height:	4", 10.1 cm
Colour:	Yellow, green and white
Issued:	1985 - 1988 (© 1985)

"KNOCKOUT BUNNYKINS"
DB 30
© ROYAL DOULTON
TABLEWARE LTD 1984

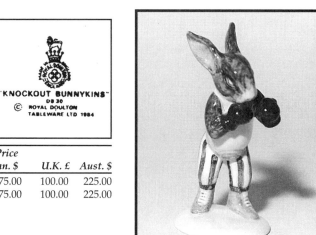

Back Stamp	Price			
	U.S. $	Can. $	U.K. £	Aust. $
BK-4	135.00	175.00	100.00	225.00
BK-5	135.00	175.00	100.00	225.00

DB31
DOWNHILL BUNNYKINS™

Designer:	Harry Sales
Modeller:	Graham Tongue
Height:	2 1/2", 6.4 cm
Colour:	Yellow, green, maroon and grey
Issued:	1985 - 1988 (© 1984)

DOWNHILL BUNNYKINS
DB 31
© ROYAL DOULTON
TABLEWARE LTD 1984

Back Stamp	Price			
	U.S. $	Can. $	U.K. £	Aust. $
BK-4	200.00	240.00	125.00	225.00
BK-5	200.00	240.00	125.00	225.00

DB32
BOGEY BUNNYKINS™

Designer:	Harry Sales
Modeller:	David Lyttleton
Height:	4", 10.1 cm
Colour:	Green, brown and yellow
Issued:	1985 - 1992 (© 1984)

"BOGEY BUNNYKINS"
DB 32
© ROYAL DOULTON
TABLEWARE LTD 1984

Back Stamp	Price			
	U.S. $	Can. $	U.K. £	Aust. $
BK-4	115.00	150.00	65.00	130.00
BK-5	115.00	150.00	65.00	130.00

DB33A
TALLY HO!™
Music Box
First Variation

Designer:	Walter Hayward
Modeller:	Albert Hallam
Height:	7", 17.8 cm
Colour:	Red coat, yellow jumper
Issued:	1984 - 1993 with "Tally Ho" figurine
Tune:	"Rock A Bye Baby"

Back Stamp	Price			
	U.S. $	Can. $	U.K. £	Aust. $
BK-4	175.00	195.00	100.00	250.00
BK-5	175.00	195.00	100.00	250.00

DB33B
TALLY HO!™
Music Box
Second Variation

Designer:	Walter Hayward
Modeller:	Albert Hallam
Height:	7", 17.8 cm
Colour:	Brown trousers, red coat and maroon tie
Issued:	1988 - 1991 with "William Bunnykins"
Tune:	"Rock A Bye Baby"

Back Stamp	Price			
	U.S. $	Can. $	U.K. £	Aust. $
BK-4	275.00	250.00	95.00	175.00
BK-5	275.00	250.00	95.00	175.00

DB34
SANTA BUNNYKINS™
Music Box

Designer:	Harry Sales
Modeller:	David Lyttleton
Height:	7 1/4", 18.4 cm
Colour:	Red, white and brown
Issued:	1984 - 1991
Tune:	"White Christmas"

Back Stamp	Price			
	U.S. $	Can. $	U.K. £	Aust. $
BK-4	175.00	195.00	85.00	175.00
BK-5	175.00	195.00	85.00	175.00

DB35
ASTRO BUNNYKINS ROCKET MAN™
Music Box

Designer:	Harry Sales
Modeller:	David Lyttleton
Height:	7", 17.8 cm
Colour:	White, red and blue
Issued:	1984 - 1989
Tune:	"Fly Me To The Moon"

Back Stamp	Price			
	U.S. $	Can. $	U.K. £	Aust. $
BK-4	225.00	250.00	115.00	220.00
BK-5	225.00	250.00	115.00	220.00

DB36
HAPPY BIRTHDAY BUNNYKINS™
Music Box

Designer:	Harry Sales
Modeller:	Graham Tongue
Height:	7", 17.8 cm
Colour:	Red and white
Issued:	1984 - 1993
Tune:	"Happy Birthday To You"

Back		Price			
Stamp		U.S. $	Can. $	U.K. £	Aust. $
BK-4		175.00	195.00	80.00	150.00
BK-5		175.00	195.00	80.00	150.00

DB37
JOGGING BUNNYKINS™
Music Box

Designer:	Harry Sales
Modeller:	David Lyttleton
Height:	5 1/2", 14.0 cm
Colour:	Yellow and blue
Issued:	1987 - 1989
Tune:	"King of the Road"

Back		Price			
Stamp		U.S. $	Can. $	U.K. £	Aust. $
BK-5		275.00	325.00	135.00	225.00

DB38
MR. BUNNYBEAT STRUMMING ™
Music Box

Designer:	Harry Sales
Modeller:	David Lyttleton
Height:	7 1/2", 19.1 cm
Colour:	Pink, white and yellow
Issued:	1987 - 1989 (©1987)
Tune:	"Hey Jude"

Back		Price			
Stamp		U.S. $	Can. $	U.K. £	Aust. $
BK-5		325.00	375.00	145.00	225.00

DB39
MRS. BUNNYKINS
AT THE EASTER PARADE™
Music Box

Designer:	Harry Sales
Modeller:	David Lyttleton
Height:	7", 17.8 cm
Colour:	Blue, yellow and maroon
Issued:	1987 - 1991 (©1988)
Tune:	"Easter Parade"

Back		Price		
Stamp	U.S. $	Can. $	U.K. £	Aust. $
BK-5	175.00	195.00	85.00	175.00

DB40
AEROBIC BUNNYKINS™

Designer:	Harry Sales
Modeller:	David Lyttleton
Height:	2 3/4", 7.0 cm
Colour:	Yellow and pale blue
Issued:	1985 - 1988 (© 1984)

Back		Price		
Stamp	U.S. $	Can. $	U.K. £	Aust. $
BK-4	200.00	275.00	100.00	225.00
BK-5	200.00	275.00	100.00	225.00

DB41
FREEFALL BUNNYKINS™

Designer:	Harry Sales
Modeller:	David Lyttleton
Height:	2 1/4", 5.7 cm
Colour:	Grey, yellow and white
Issued:	1986 - 1989 (© 1984)

Back		Price		
Stamp	U.S. $	Can. $	U.K. £	Aust. $
BK-4	225.00	275.00	150.00	235.00
BK-5	225.00	275.00	150.00	235.00

DB42
ACE BUNNYKINS™

Designer: Harry Sales
Modeller: David Lyttleton
Height: 3 3/4", 9.5 cm
Colour: White and blue
Issued: 1986 - 1989 (© 1985)

Back Stamp	U.S. $	Price Can. $	U.K. £	Aust. $
BK-4	200.00	295.00	115.00	235.00
BK-5	200.00	295.00	115.00	235.00

DB43
HOME RUN BUNNYKINS™
(1 on Back of Jersey)

Designer: Harry Sales
Modeller: David Lyttleton
Height: 4", 10.1 cm
Colour: Blue, yellow and white
Issued: 1986 - 1993 (© 1985)

Back Stamp	U.S. $	Price Can. $	U.K. £	Aust. $
BK-4	75.00	95.00	30.00	125.00
BK-5	75.00	95.00	30.00	125.00

Note: The number DB 44 was assigned to the figurine Ballet Bunnykins; however, this figure was never issued.

DB45
KING JOHN™
First Variation

Designer: Harry Sales
Modeller: David Lyttleton
Height: 4", 10.1 cm
Colour: Red, yellow and blue
Issued: 1986 - 1990 (© 1985)
Varieties: DB91
Series: Bunnykins Royal Family

Back Stamp	U.S. $	Price Can. $	U.K. £	Aust. $
BK-4	100.00	150.00	55.00	200.00
BK-5	100.00	150.00	55.00	200.00
Set DB45 - 49 (5 pcs.)	400.00	500.00	275.00	1,000.00

Royal Doulton News

Store Specializes in Discontinued

Characters Look For New Home

Marine City, MI.: With an entire store full of Royal Doulton, people often look to *Seaway China* in Marine City, MI to find that special discontinued Beatrix Potter, Bunnykins, Brambly Hedge, or Snowman. Hundreds of Royal Doulton collectors count on *Seaway* to locate their special needs. In addition to their own 32 page color catalog, *Seaway* can mail or fax special lists of Royal Doulton Collectibles. *Seaway China* are specialists in discontinued figures and character jugs.

    For more information call **1-800-968-2424**.

Shown above are a collection of Bunnykins at Seaway China. Call Seaway China at 1-800-968-2424 for more information about Bunnykins.

DB46
QUEEN SOPHIE™
First Variation

Designer:	Harry Sales
Modeller:	David Lyttleton
Height:	4 1/2", 11.4 cm
Colour:	Blue and red
Issued:	1986 - 1990 (© 1985)
Varieties:	DB92
Series:	Bunnykins Royal Family

Back Stamp	Price U.S. $	Can. $	U.K. £	Aust. $
BK-4	100.00	115.00	55.00	200.00
BK-5	100.00	115.00	55.00	200.00

DB47
PRINCESS BEATRICE™
First Variation

Designer:	Harry Sales
Modeller:	David Lyttleton
Height:	3 1/2", 8.9 cm
Colour:	Pale green
Issued:	1986 - 1990 (© 1985)
Varieties:	DB93
Series:	Bunnykins Royal Family

Back Stamp	Price U.S. $	Can. $	U.K. £	Aust. $
BK-4	85.00	110.00	45.00	200.00
BK-5	85.00	110.00	45.00	200.00

DB48
PRINCE FREDERICK™
First Variation

Designer:	Harry Sales
Modeller:	David Lyttleton
Height:	3 1/2", 8.9 cm
Colour:	Green, white and red
Issued:	1986 - 1990 (© 1985)
Varieties:	DB94
Series:	Bunnykins Royal Family

Back Stamp	Price U.S. $	Can. $	U.K. £	Aust. $
BK-4	95.00	135.00	45.00	200.00
BK-5	95.00	135.00	45.00	200.00

DB49
HARRY THE HERALD™
First Variation

Designer:	Harry Sales
Modeller:	David Lyttleton
Height:	3 1/2", 8.9 cm
Colour:	Maroon, white and tan
Issued:	1986 - 1990 (© 1985)
Varieties:	DB95, DB115
Series:	Bunnykins Royal Family

Back		Price		
Stamp	U.S. $	Can. $	U.K. £	Aust. $
BK-4	110.00	135.00	80.00	200.00
BK-5	110.00	135.00	80.00	200.00

DB50
UNCLE SAM BUNNYKINS™

Designer:	Harry Sales
Modeller:	David Lyttleton
Height:	4 1/2", 11 cm
Colour:	Blue, red and white
Issued:	1986 to the present (© 1985)

Back		Price		
Stamp	U.S. $	Can. $	U.K. £	Aust. $
BK-4	40.00	60.00	30.00	100.00
BK-5	40.00	60.00	30.00	100.00

Note: Made exclusively for the U.S. market.

DB51
MR. BUNNYKINS AT THE EASTER PARADE ™
Second Variation

Designer:	Harry Sales
Modeller:	David Lyttleton
Height:	5", 12.7 cm
Colour:	Blue tie and hat band, maroon coat, light grey trousers, pink ribbon on package
Issued:	1986 - 1986
Varieties:	DB18

Back		Price		
Stamp	U.S. $	Can. $	U.K. £	Aust. $
BK-Special	750.00	800.00	325.00	900.00

Note: Made exclusively for distribution in the U.S. market at Beswick artist events.

DB52
MRS. BUNNYKINS AT THE
EASTER PARADE™
Second Variation

Designer:	Harry Sales
Modeller:	David Lyttleton
Height:	4 1/2", 11.4 cm
Colour:	Maroon dress, white collar, blue bow on bonnet, multi-coloured bows on packages
Issued:	1986 - 1986
Varieties:	DB19

Back Stamp	U.S. $	Can. $	Price U.K. £	Aust. $
BK-Special	850.00	900.00	375.00	900.00

Note: Made exclusively for distribution in the U.S. market at Beswick artist events.

DB53
CAROL SINGER™
Music Box

Designer:	Harry Sales
Modeller:	David Lyttleton
Height:	7", 17.8 cm
Colour:	Red, yellow and green
Issued:	1986 - 1989
Tune:	"Silent Night"

Back Stamp	U.S. $	Can. $	Price U.K. £	Aust. $
BK-4	175.00	250.00	135.00	235.00
BK-5	175.00	250.00	135.00	235.00

DB54
COLLECTOR BUNNYKINS™

Designer:	Harry Sales
Modeller:	David Lyttleton
Height:	4 1/4", 10.8 cm
Colour:	Brown, blue and grey
Issued:	1987 - 1987
Series:	R.D.I.C.C.

INTERNATIONAL COLLECTORS CLUB
ROYAL DOULTON

COLLECTOR BUNNYKINS
D854
EXCLUSIVELY FOR
COLLECTORS CLUB
© 1986 ROYAL DOULTON
MODELLED BY
D Lyttleton

Back Stamp	U.S. $	Can. $	Price U.K. £	Aust. $
BK-Special	750.00	850.00	475.00	950.00

DB55
BEDTIME BUNNYKINS™
First Variation

Designer:	Graham Tongue
Modeller:	David Lyttleton
Height:	3 1/4", 8.3 cm
Colour:	Blue and white striped pyjamas, brown teddy bear
Issued:	1987 to the present (© 1986)
Varieties:	DB63, 79, 103

Back Stamp	Price			
	U.S. $	Can. $	U.K. £	Aust. $
BK-5	40.00	58.50	14.95	60.00

DB56
BE PREPARED BUNNYKINS™

Designer:	Graham Tongue
Modeller:	David Lyttleton
Height:	4", 10.1 cm
Colour:	Dark green and grey
Issued:	1987 to the present (© 1986)

Back Stamp	Price			
	U.S. $	Can. $	U.K. £	Aust. $
BK-5	40.00	58.50	14.95	69.00

DB57
SCHOOL DAYS BUNNYKINS™

Designer:	Graham Tongue
Modeller:	David Lyttleton
Height:	3 1/2", 8.9 cm
Colour:	Dark green, white and yellow
Issued:	1987 - 1995 (© 1986)

Back Stamp	Price			
	U.S. $	Can. $	U.K. £	Aust. $
BK-5	60.00	75.00	25.00	79.00

DB58
AUSTRALIAN BUNNYKINS™

Designer: Harry Sales
Modeller: Warren Platt
Height: 4", 10.1 cm
Colour: Gold and green
Issued: 1988 - 1988

Back Stamp	U.S. $	Can. $	U.K. £	Aust. $
BK-Special	450.00	400.00	175.00	500.00

Note: Sold exclusively in Australia to celebrate the Australian bicentenary.

DB59
STORYTIME BUNNYKINS™
Second Variation

Designer: Walter Hayward
Modeller: Albert Hallam
Height: 3", 7.6 cm
Colour: Left — green polka dots on
white dress, yellow shoes
Right — yellow dress, green shoes
Issued: 1987 - 1987 (© 1974)
Varieties: DB9; also called "Partners in Collecting," DB151

Back Stamp	U.S. $	Can. $	U.K. £	Aust. $
BK-Special	400.00	425.00	150.00	350.00

Note: Produced for distribution at special events in the U.S.A.

DB60
SCHOOLMASTER BUNNYKINS™

Designer: Graham Tongue
Modeller: Warren Platt
Height: 4", 10 cm
Colour: Black, white, green
and white
Issued: 1987 to the present
(© 1987)

Back Stamp	U.S. $	Can. $	U.K. £	Aust. $
BK-5	50.00	58.50	15.95	95.00

DB61
BROWNIE BUNNYKINS™

Designer:	Graham Tongue
Modeller:	Warren Platt
Height:	4", 10 cm
Colour:	Brown uniform, yellow neck-tie
Issued:	1987 - 1993 (© 1987)

Back Stamp	Price			
	U.S. $	Can. $	U.K. £	Aust. $
BK-5	65.00	85.00	30.00	95.00

DB62
SANTA BUNNYKINS HAPPY CHRISTMAS™
Christmas Tree Ornament

Designer:	Harry Sales
Modeller:	David Lyttleton
Height:	Unknown
Colour:	Red and white
Issued:	1987 in a limited edition of 1551

Back Stamp	Price			
	U.S. $	Can. $	U.K. £	Aust. $
BK-Special	1,600.00	1,700.00	900.00	1,750.00

DB63
BEDTIME BUNNYKINS™
Second Variation

Designer:	Graham Tongue
Modeller:	David Lyttleton
Height:	3 1/4", 8.3 cm
Colour:	Red and white striped pyjamas, white teddy bear
Issued:	1987 - 1987 (© 1986)
Varieties:	DB55, 79, 103

Back Stamp	Price			
	U.S. $	Can. $	U.K. £	Aust. $
BK-Special	300.00	275.00	140.00	350.00

Note: Commissioned by D.H. Holmes, New Orleans, Louisiana.

DB64
POLICEMAN BUNNYKINS™

Designer:	Graham Tongue
Modeller:	Martyn Alcock
Height:	4 1/4", 10.8 cm
Colour:	Dark blue uniform
Issued:	1988 to the present
	(© 1987)

Back		Price		
Stamp	U.S. $	Can. $	U.K. £	Aust. $
BK-5	40.00	49.00	14.95	69.00

DB65
LOLLIPOPMAN BUNNYKINS™

Designer:	Graham Tongue
Modeller:	Martyn Alcock
Height:	3 3/4", 9.5 cm
Colour:	White and yellow
Issued:	1988 - 1991
	(reg'd 1987)

Back		Price		
Stamp	U.S. $	Can. $	U.K. £	Aust. $
BK-5	90.00	135.00	60.00	175.00

DB66
SCHOOLBOY BUNNYKINS™

Designer:	Graham Tongue
Modeller:	Martyn Alcock
Height:	4", 10.1 cm
Colour:	Blue, white and grey
Issued:	1988 - 1991 (© 1987)

Back		Price		
Stamp	U.S. $	Can. $	U.K. £	Aust. $
BK-5	90.00	200.00	60.00	175.00

DB67
FAMILY PHOTOGRAPH BUNNYKINS™
Second Variation

Designer:	Walter Hayward
Modeller:	Albert Hallam
Height:	4 1/2", 11.4 cm
Colour:	Pink , black and white
Issued:	1988 - 1988 (©1972)
Varieties:	DB1; also called "Father, Mother and Victoria Bunnykins," DB68

Back Stamp	Price			
	U.S. $	Can. $	U.K. £	Aust. $
BK-Special	225.00	195.00	85.00	250.00

Note: A new colourway was produced in 1988 for special events in the U.S.A.

DB68
FATHER, MOTHER AND VICTORIA BUNNYKINS™

Designer:	Based on design "Family Photograph" by Walter Hayward
Modeller:	Martyn Alcock
Height:	4 1/2", 11.4 cm
Colour:	Blue, grey, maroon and yellow
Issued:	1988 to the present (© 1988)
Varieties:	Also called "Family Photograph," DB1, 67

Back Stamp	Price			
	U.S. $	Can. $	U.K. £	Aust. $
BK-5	50.00	58.50	16.95	95.00

DB69
WILLIAM BUNNYKINS™

Designer:	Based on design by Walter Hayward
Modeller:	Martyn Alcock
Height:	Unknown
Colour:	Red and white
Issued:	1988 - 1993
Varieties:	Also called "Tally Ho! Bunnykins," DB 12, 78

Back Stamp	Price			
	U.S. $	Can. $	U.K. £	Aust. $
BK-5	75.00	95.00	35.00	100.00

DB70
SUSAN BUNNYKINS™

Designer:	Based on a design by Walter Hayward
Modeller:	Martyn Alcock
Height:	3 1/4", 8.3 cm
Colour:	White, blue and yellow
Issued:	1988 - 1993 (© 1988)

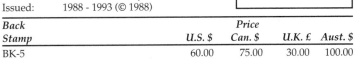

Back Stamp	Price			
	U.S. $	Can. $	U.K. £	Aust. $
BK-5	60.00	75.00	30.00	100.00

DB71
POLLY BUNNYKINS™

Designer:	Graham Tongue
Modeller:	Martyn Alcock
Height:	3 1/2", 8.7 cm
Colour:	Pink
Issued:	1988 - 1993 (© 1988)

Back Stamp	Price			
	U.S. $	Can. $	U.K. £	Aust. $
BK-5	60.00	75.00	30.00	100.00

DB72
TOM BUNNYKINS™

Designer:	Graham Tongue
Modeller:	Martyn Alcock
Height:	3", 7.6 cm
Colour:	Browns, white and blue
Issued:	1988 - 1993 (© 1988)

Back Stamp	Price			
	U.S. $	Can. $	U.K. £	Aust. $
BK-5	60.00	75.00	30.00	100.00

DB73
HARRY BUNNYKINS™

Designer:	Graham Tongue
Modeller:	Martyn Alcock
Height:	3", 7.9 cm
Colour:	Blue, brown, white and yellow
Issued:	1988 - 1993 (© 1988)

Back Stamp	U.S. $	Price Can. $	U.K. £	Aust. $
BK-5	60.00	75.00	25.00	100.00

DB74A
NURSE BUNNYKINS™
First Variation (Red Cross)

Designer:	Graham Tongue
Modeller:	Martyn Alcock
Height:	4 1/4", 10.8 cm
Colour:	Dark and light blue and white, red cross
Issued:	1989 - 1994 (© 1988)
Varieties:	DB 74B

Back Stamp	U.S. $	Price Can. $	U.K. £	Aust. $
BK-5	165.00	195.00	85.00	220.00

DB74B
NURSE BUNNYKINS™
Second Variation (Green Cross)

Designer:	Graham Tongue
Modeller:	Martyn Alcock
Height:	4 1/4", 10.8 cm
Colour:	Dark and light blue and white, green cross
Issued:	1989 to the present (© 1988)
Varieties:	DB 74A

Back Stamp	U.S. $	Price Can. $	U.K. £	Aust. $
BK-5	40.00	52.00	14.95	75.00

DB75
FIREMAN BUNNYKINS™

Designer:	Graham Tongue
Modeller:	Martyn Alcock
Height:	4 1/4", 10.8 cm
Colour:	Dark blue and yellow
Issued:	1989 to the present (© 1988)

| Back Stamp | Price | | | |
	U.S. $	Can. $	U.K. £	Aust. $
BK-5	40.00	58.50	15.95	69.00

DB76
POSTMAN BUNNYKINS™

Designer:	Graham Tongue
Modeller:	Martyn Alcock
Height:	4 1/2", 11.4 cm
Colour:	Dark blue and red
Issued:	1989 - 1993 (© 1989)

| Back Stamp | Price | | | |
	U.S. $	Can. $	U.K. £	Aust. $
BK-5	75.00	90.00	40.00	125.00

DB77
PAPERBOY BUNNYKINS™

Designer:	Graham Tongue
Modeller:	Martyn Alcock
Height:	4", 10.4 cm
Colour:	Green, yellow, red and white
Issued:	1989 - 1993

| Back Stamp | Price | | | |
	U.S. $	Can. $	U.K. £	Aust. $
BK-5	75.00	95.00	40.00	125.00

DB78
TALLY HO! BUNNYKINS™
Second Variation

Designer:	Based on a design by Walter Hayward
Modeller:	Albert Hallam
Height:	4", 9.8 cm
Colour:	Light blue coat and white rocking horse, yellow sweater
Issued:	1988 - 1988 (© 1974)
Varieties:	DB12; also called "William Bunnykins," DB69

Back Stamp	Price U.S. $	Can. $	U.K. £	Aust. $
BK-Special	225.00	250.00	70.00	225.00

Note: Commissioned by Macy's Department Store, New York, N.Y. Also painted in deeper shades of blue and yellow.

DB79
BEDTIME BUNNYKINS™
Third Variation

Designer:	Graham Tongue
Modeller:	David Lyttleton
Height:	3 1/4", 8.3 cm
Colour:	Light blue and white
Issued:	1988 - 1988
Varieties:	DB55, 63, 103

Back Stamp	Price U.S. $	Can. $	U.K. £	Aust. $
BK-Special	300.00	375.00	185.00	350.00

Note: Issued for the 100th anniversary of Belk, 1888 - 1988.

DB80
DOLLIE BUNNYKINS PLAYTIME ™
Second Variation

Designer:	Based on a design by Walter Hayward
Modeller:	Albert Hallam
Height:	4", 10.1 cm
Colour:	White and yellow
Issued:	1988 - 1988 (© 1972)
Varieties:	DB8

Back Stamp	Type	Price U.S. $	Can. $	U.K. £	Aust. $
BK-Special "Higbee"		250.00	325.00	75.00	225.00
BK-Special "Holmes "		250.00	325.00	75.00	225.00
BK-Special "Hornes"		250.00	325.00	75.00	225.00
BK-Special "Strawbridge"		250.00	325.00	75.00	225.00

Note: Issued for the Doulton Rooms in the U.S.A.; 250 in each edition.

DB81
BILLIE AND BUNTIE BUNNYKINS
SLEIGH RIDE™
Second Variation

Designer:	Based on a design by Walter Hayward
Modeller:	Albert Hallam
Height:	3 1/2", 8.9 cm
Colour:	Green, yellow and red
Issued:	1989 - 1989 (© 1972)
Varieties:	DB4

Back Stamp	Price U.S. $	Can. $	U.K. £	Aust. $
BK-Special	175.00	225.00	90.00	200.00

Note: This model was created for the special events tour in 1989.

DB82
ICE CREAM BUNNYKINS™

Designer:	Graham Tongue
Modeller:	Warren Platt
Height:	4 1/2", 11.4 cm
Colour:	White, blue and green
Issued:	1990 - 1993 (©1989)

Back Stamp	Price U.S. $	Can. $	U.K. £	Aust. $
BK-5	90.00	100.00	45.00	135.00

DB83
SUSAN BUNNYKINS AS
QUEEN OF THE MAY™

Designer:	Graham Tongue
Modeller:	Martyn Alcock
Height:	4", 10.2 cm
Colour:	White polka-dot dress, blue and brown chair
Issued:	1990 - 1991 (© 1989)

Back Stamp	Price U.S. $	Can. $	U.K. £	Aust. $
BK-5	150.00	125.00	45.00	145.00

DB84
FISHERMAN BUNNYKINS™

Designer:	Graham Tongue
Modeller:	Warren Platt
Height:	4 1/4", 10.8 cm
Colour:	Maroon, yellow and grey
Issued:	1990 - 1993 (© 1990)

Back Stamp	Price			
	U.S. $	Can. $	U.K. £	Aust. $
BK-5	100.00	120.00	40.00	135.00

DB85
COOK BUNNYKINS™

Designer:	Graham Tongue
Modeller:	Warren Platt
Height:	4 1/4", 10.8 cm
Colour:	White and green
Issued:	1990 - 1995 (© 1990)

Back Stamp	Price			
	U.S. $	Can. $	U.K. £	Aust. $
BK-5	65.00	75.00	30.00	135.00

DB86
SOUSAPHONE BUNNYKINS™
From the Oompah Band - Second Variation

Designer:	Harry Sales
Modeller:	David Lyttleton
Height:	3 1/2", 8.9 cm
Colour:	Blue uniform and yellow sousaphone
Issued:	1990 in a limited edition of 250 sets (© 1990)
Series:	Royal Doulton Collectors Band
Varieties:	DB23, 105

Back Stamp	Price			
	U.S. $	Can. $	U.K. £	Aust. $
BK-U.K. Fairs	200.00	225.00	100.00	400.00
DB86 to 90 (5 pcs.)	1,000.00	1,125.00	500.00	2,000.00

Note: Special colourway edition of 250. Exclusive for U.K. Fairs Ltd.

DB87
TRUMPETER BUNNYKINS™
From the Oompah Band - Second Variation

Designer:	Harry Sales
Modeller:	David Lyttleton
Height:	3 3/4", 9.5 cm
Colour:	Blue uniform and yellow trumpet
Issued:	1990 in a limited edition of 250 sets
Series:	Royal Doulton Collectors Band
Varieties:	DB24, 106

Back Stamp	Price			
	U.S. $	Can. $	U.K. £	Aust. $
BK-Special	200.00	225.00	100.00	400.00

Note: Special colourway edition of 250. Exclusive for U.K. Fairs Ltd.

DB88
CYMBALS BUNNYKINS™
From the Oompah Band - Second Variation

Designer:	Harry Sales
Modeller:	David Lyttleton
Height:	3 1/2", 8.9 cm
Colour:	Blue uniform and yellow cymbals
Issued:	1990 in a limited edition of 250 sets
Series:	Royal Doulton Collectors Band
Varieties:	DB25, 107

Back Stamp	Price			
	U.S. $	Can. $	U.K. £	Aust. $
BK-Special	200.00	225.00	100.00	400.00

Note: Special colourway edition of 250. Exclusive for U.K. Fairs Ltd.

DB89
DRUMMER BUNNYKINS
Third Variation

Designer:	Harry Sales
Modeller:	David Lyttleton
Height:	3 3/4", 9.5 cm
Colour:	Blue trousers and sleeves, yellow vest, cream and red drum
Issued:	1990 in a limited edition of 250 sets (© 1990)
Series:	Royal Doulton Collectors Band
Varieties:	DB26, 26A, 26B, 108

Back Stamp	Price			
	U.S. $	Can. $	U.K. £	Aust. $
BK-Special	200.00	225.00	100.00	400.00

Note: Special colourway edition of 250. Exclusive for U.K. Fairs Ltd.

DB90
DRUM-MAJOR BUNNYKINS™
Second Variation

Designer:	Harry Sales
Modeller:	David Lyttleton
Height:	3 3/4", 9.5 cm
Colour:	Blue and yellow uniform
Issued:	1990 in a limited edition of 250 sets
Series:	Royal Doulton Collectors Band
Varieties:	DB27, 109

Back Stamp	Price			
	U.S. $	Can. $	U.K. £	Aust. $
BK-Special	200.00	225.00	100.00	400.00

Note: Special colourway edition of 250. Exclusive for U.K. Fairs Ltd.

DB91
KING JOHN™
Second Variation

Designer:	Harry Sales
Modeller:	David Lyttleton
Height:	4", 10.1 cm
Colour:	Purple, yellow and white
Issued:	1990 in a limited edition of 250 sets (© 1990)
Series:	Bunnykins Royal Family
Varieties:	DB45

Back Stamp	Price			
	U.S. $	Can. $	U.K. £	Aust. $
BK-Special	200.00	325.00	85.00	400.00
Set DB91 - 95 (5 Pcs)	1,000.00	1,500.00	425.00	2,000.00

Note: Exclusive colourway of 250 sets for U.K. International Ceramics Ltd.

DB92
QUEEN SOPHIE™
Second Variation

Designer:	Harry Sales
Modeller:	David Lyttleton
Height:	4 1/2", 11.4 cm
Colour:	Pink and purple
Issued:	1990 in a limited edition of 250 (© 1990)
Series:	Bunnykins Royal Family
Varieties:	DB46

Back Stamp	Price			
	U.S. $	Can. $	U.K. £	Aust. $
BK-Special	200.00	325.00	85.00	400.00

Note: Exclusive colourway of 250 sets for U.K. International Ceramics Ltd.

DB93
PRINCESS BEATRICE™
Second Variation

Designer:	Harry Sales
Modeller:	David Lyttleton
Height:	3 1/2", 8.9 cm
Colour:	Yellow and gold
Issued:	1990 in a limited edition of 250 (© 1990)
Series:	Bunnykins Royal Family
Varieties:	DB47

Back Stamp	Price			
	U.S. $	Can. $	U.K. £	Aust. $
BK-Special	200.00	325.00	85.00	400.00

Note: Exclusive colourway of 250 sets for U.K. International Ceramics Ltd.

DB94
PRINCE FREDERICK™
Second Variation

Designer:	Harry Sales
Modeller:	David Lyttleton
Height:	3 1/2", 8.9 cm
Colour:	Red, blue and yellow
Issued:	1990 in a limited edition of 250 (© 1990)
Series:	Bunnykins Royal Family
Varieties:	DB48

Back Stamp	Price			
	U.S. $	Can. $	U.K. £	Aust. $
BK-Special	200.00	175.00	85.00	400.00

Note: Exclusive colourway of 250 sets for U.K. International Ceramics Ltd.

DB95
HARRY THE HERALD™
Second Variation

Designer:	Harry Sales
Modeller:	David Lyttleton
Height:	3 1/2", 8.9 cm
Colour:	Blue, red and yellow
Issued:	1990 in a limited edition of 250 (© 1990)
Series:	Bunnykins Royal Family
Varieties:	DB49, 115

Back Stamp	Price			
	U.S. $	Can. $	U.K. £	Aust. $
BK-Special	200.00	175.00	85.00	400.00

Note: Exclusive colourway of 250 sets for U.K. International Ceramics Ltd.

DB96
TOUCHDOWN BUNNYKINS™
Third Variation (Ohio State University)

Designer:	Harry Sales
Modeller:	David Lyttleton
Height:	3 1/4", 8.3 cm
Colour:	Grey and orange
Issued:	1990
Varieties:	DB29, 29A, 29B, 97, 98, 99, 100

Back	Price			
Stamp	U.S. $	Can. $	U.K. £	Aust. $
BK-Special	135.00	175.00	75.00	500.00
Set, DB96-100 (5 pcs)	675.00	875.00	375.00	2,500.00

Note: Issued in a limited edition of 200.

DB97
TOUCHDOWN BUNNYKINS™
Fourth Variation (University of Michigan)

Designer:	Harry Sales
Modeller:	David Lyttleton
Height:	3 1/4", 8.3 cm
Colour:	Yellow and blue
Issued:	1990
Varieties:	DB29, 96, 98, 99, 100

Back	Price			
Stamp	U.S. $	Can. $	U.K. £	Aust. $
BK-Special	135.00	175.00	75.00	500.00

Note: Issued in a limited edition of 200.

DB98
TOUCHDOWN BUNNYKINS™
Fifth Variation (Cincinnati Bengals)

Designer:	Harry Sales
Modeller:	David Lyttleton
Height:	3 1/2", 8.3 cm
Colour:	Orange and black
Issued:	1990 (©1990)
Varieties:	DB29, 96, 97, 99, 100

Back	Price			
Stamp	U.S. $	Can. $	U.K. £	Aust. $
BK-Special	135.00	175.00	75.00	500.00

Note: Issued in a limited edition of 200.

DB99
TOUCHDOWN BUNNYKINS™
Sixth Variation (Notre Dame College)

Designer:	Harry Sales
Modeller:	David Lyttleton
Height:	3 1/2", 8.3 cm
Colour:	Green and yellow
Issued:	1990 (©1990)
Varieties:	DB29, 96, 97, 98, 100

Back Stamp	Price U.S. $	Can. $	U.K. £	Aust. $
BK-Special	135.00	175.00	75.00	500.00

Note: Issued in a limited edition of 200.

DB100
TOUCHDOWN BUNNYKINS™
Seventh Variation (University of Indiana)

Designer:	Harry Sales
Modeller:	David Lyttleton
Height:	3 1/2", 8.3 cm
Colour:	White and red
Issued:	1990 (©1990)
Varieties:	DB29, 96, 97, 98, 99

Back Stamp	Price U.S. $	Can. $	U.K. £	Aust. $
BK-Special	135.00	175.00	75.00	500.00

Note: Issued in a limited edition of 200.

DB101
BRIDE BUNNYKINS™

Designer:	Graham Tongue
Modeller:	Amanda Hughes-Lubeck
Height:	4", 10.1 cm
Colour:	Cream dress, grey, blue and white train
Issued:	1991 to the present (©1990)

Back Stamp	Price U.S. $	Can. $	U.K. £	Aust. $
BK-5	40.00	66.00	16.95	64.00

DB102
GROOM BUNNYKINS™

Designer:	Graham Tongue
Modeller:	Martyn Alcock
Height:	4 1/2", 11.4 cm
Colour:	Grey and burgundy
Issued:	1991 to the present (©1990)

Back		Price		
Stamp	U.S. $	Can. $	U.K. £	Aust. $
BK-5	40.00	66.00	16.95	64.00

DB103
BEDTIME BUNNYKINS™
Fourth Variation

Designer:	Graham Tongue
Modeller:	David Lyttelton
Height:	3 1/4", 8.3 cm
Colour:	Yellow and green striped pyjamas, brown teddy bear
Issued:	1991 - 1991 (©1986)
Varieties:	DB55, 63, 79

Back		Price		
Stamp	Type	U.S. $	Can. $	U.K. £	Aust. $
BK-Special Pale yellow	225.00	275.00	100.00	225.00
BK-Special Daffodil yellow	225.00	275.00	100.00	225.00

Note: Issued for the U.S. special events tour in 1991.

DB104
CAROL SINGER BUNNYKINS™

Designer:	Harry Sales
Modeller:	David Lyttleton
Height:	4", 10.1 cm
Colour:	Dark green, red, yellow and white
Issued:	1991 (© 1986)

Back		Price		
Stamp	U.S. $	Can. $	U.K.£	Aust. $
BK-Special, DB104A	125.00	150.00	45.00	230.00
BK-Special, DB104B	175.00	200.00	65.00	500.00

Note: Issued in a special edition of 1,000, exclusively for U.K. International Ceramics Ltd. 300 of the edition (DB104B) have U.S.A. on the backstamp.

DB105
SOUSAPHONE BUNNYKINS™
From the Oompah Band - Third Variation

Designer:	Harry Sales
Modeller:	David Lyttleton
Height:	4", 10.1 cm
Colour:	Dark green, red and yellow
Issued:	1991 (© 1991)
Series:	Royal Doulton Collectors Band
Varieties:	DB 23, 86

Back Stamp	Price U.S. $	Can. $	U.K. £	Aust. $
BK-Special	200.00	225.00	75.00	400.00
Set DB 105 to 109 (5 pcs.)	1,000.00	1,100.00	375.00	2,000.00

Note: Issued in a special edition of 250, exclusive to U.K. Int'l Ceramics Ltd.

DB106
TRUMPETER BUNNYKINS™
From the Oompah Band - Third Variation

Designer:	Harry Sales
Modeller:	David Lyttleton
Height:	3 3/4", 9.5 cm
Colour:	Dark green, red and yellow
Issued:	1991 (© 1991)
Series:	Royal Doulton Collectors Band
Varieties:	DB 24, 87

Back Stamp	Price U.S. $	Can. $	U.K. £	Aust. $
BK-Special	200.00	225.00	75.00	400.00

Note: Issued in a special edition of 250, exclusive to U.K. Int'l Ceramics Ltd.

DB107
CYMBALS BUNNYKINS™
From the Oompah Band - Third Variation

Designer:	Harry Sales
Modeller:	David Lyttleton
Height:	4", 10.1 cm
Colour:	Dark green, red and yellow
Issued:	1991 (© 1991)
Series:	Royal Doulton Collectors Band
Varieties:	DB 25, 88

Back Stamp	Price U.S. $	Can. $	U.K. £	Aust. $
BK-Special	200.00	225.00	75.00	400.00

Note: Issued in a special edition of 250, exclusive to U.K. Int'l Ceramics Ltd.

DB 108
DRUMMER BUNNYKINS™
From the Oompah Band - Fourth Variation

Designer:	Harry Sales
Modeller:	David Lyttleton
Height:	3 1/2", 8.9 cm
Colour:	Dark green, red and white
Issued:	1991 (© 1991)
Series:	Royal Doulton Collectors Band
Varieties:	DB 26, 26A, 26B, 89

Back Stamp	Price			
	U.S. $	Can. $	U.K. £	Aust. $
BK-Special	200.00	225.00	75.00	400.00

Note: Special colourway edition of 250, exclusive to U.K. Fairs Ltd.

DB 109
DRUM-MAJOR BUNNYKINS™
From the Oompah Band - Third Variation

Designer:	Harry Sales
Modeller:	David Lyttleton
Height:	3 1/2", 8.9 cm
Colour:	Dark green, red and yellow
Issued:	1991 (© 1991)
Series:	Royal Doulton Collectors Band
Varieties:	DB 27, 90

Back Stamp	Price			
	U.S. $	Can. $	U.K. £	Aust. $
BK-Special	200.00	225.00	75.00	400.00

Note: Special colourway edition of 250, exclusive to U.K. Int'l Ceramics Ltd.

Note: DB 110 to 114 were not issued.

DB115
HARRY THE HERALD™
Third Variation

Designer:	Harry Sales
Modeller:	David Lyttleton
Height:	3 1/2", 8.9 cm
Colour:	Yellow and dark blue
Issued:	1991 (© 1991)
Series:	Bunnykins Royal Family
Varieties:	DB 49, 95

Back Stamp	Price			
	U.S. $	Can. $	U.K. £	Aust. $
BK-Special	400.00	500.00	300.00	600.00

Note: Commissioned by Lambeth Productions in a special edition of 300.

DB116
GOALKEEPER BUNNYKINS ™
First Variation

Designer:	Denise Andrews
Modeller:	Warren Platt
Height:	4 1/2", 11.4 cm
Colour:	Green and black
Issued:	1991 (© 1991)
Series:	Footballers
Varieties:	DB 118, 120, 122

Back Stamp	Price			
	U.S. $	Can. $	U.K. £	Aust. $
BK-Special	150.00	200.00	75.00	500.00

Note: Special edition of 250, exclusive to U.K. International Ceramics Ltd.

DB117
FOOTBALLER BUNNYKINS™
First Variation

Designer:	Denise Andrews
Modeller:	Warren Platt
Height:	4 1/2", 11.4 cm
Colour:	Green and white
Issued:	1991 (© 1991)
Series:	Footballers
Varieties:	DB 119, 121; also called "Soccer Player," DB123

Back Stamp	Price			
	U.S. $	Can. $	U.K. £	Aust. $
BK-Special	150.00	200.00	75.00	500.00

Note: Special edition of 250, exclusive to U.K. International Ceramics Ltd.

DB118
GOALKEEPER BUNNYKINS ™
Second Variation

Designer:	Denise Andrews
Modeller:	Warren Platt
Height:	4 1/2", 11.4 cm
Colour:	Red and black
Issued:	1991 (© 1991)
Series:	Footballers
Varieties:	DB 116, 120, 122

Back Stamp	Price			
	U.S. $	Can. $	U.K. £	Aust. $
BK-Special	150.00	200.00	75.00	500.00

Note: Special edition of 250, exclusive to U.K. International Ceramics Ltd.

DB119
FOOTBALLER BUNNYKINS ™
Second Variation

Designer:	Denise Andrews
Modeller:	Warren Platt
Height:	4 1/2", 11.4 cm
Colour:	Red
Issued:	1991 (© 1991)
Series:	Footballers
Varieties:	DB 117, 121; also called "Soccer Player," DB123

Back Stamp	Price			
	U.S. $	Can. $	U.K. £	Aust. $
BK-Special	150.00	200.00	75.00	500.00

Note: Special edition of 250, exclusive to U.K. International Ceramics Ltd.

DB120
GOALKEEPER BUNNYKINS ™
Third Variation

Designer:	Denise Andrews
Modeller:	Warren Platt
Height:	4 1/2", 11.4 cm
Colour:	Yellow and black
Issued:	1991 (© 1991)
Series:	Footballers
Varieties:	DB 116, 118, 122

Back Stamp	Price			
	U.S. $	Can. $	U.K. £	Aust. $
BK-Special	150.00	200.00	75.00	500.00

Note: Special edition of 250, exclusive to U.K. International Ceramics Ltd.

DB121
FOOTBALLER BUNNYKINS ™
Third Variation

Designer:	Denise Andrews
Modeller:	Warren Platt
Height:	4 1/2", 11.4 cm
Colour:	White and blue
Issued:	1991 (© 1991)
Series:	Footballers
Varieties:	DB 117, 119; also called "Soccer Player," DB123

Back Stamp	Price			
	U.S. $	Can. $	U.K. £	Aust. $
BK-Special	150.00	200.00	75.00	500.00

Note: Special edition of 250, exclusive to U.K. International Ceramics Ltd.

DB122
GOALKEEPER BUNNYKINS ™
Fourth Variation

Designer:	Denise Andrews
Modeller:	Warren Platt
Height:	4 1/2", 1.4 cm
Colour:	Grey and black
Issued:	1991 (©1991)
Series:	Footballers
Varieties:	DB 118, 118, 120

Back	Price			
Stamp	U.S. $	Can. $	U.K. £	Aust. $
BK-Special	150.00	200.00	75.00	500.00

Note: Special edition of 250, exclusive to U.K. International Ceramics Ltd.

DB123
SOCCER PLAYER BUNNYKINS ™

Designer:	Denise Andrews
Modeller:	Warren Platt
Height:	4 1/2", 11.4 cm
Colour:	Dark blue and white
Issued:	1991 (© 1991)
Series:	Footballers
Varieties:	Also called "Footballer Bunnykins," DB 117, 119, 121

Back	Price			
Stamp	U.S. $	Can. $	U.K. £	Aust. $
BK-Special	150.00	200.00	75.00	500.00

Note: Special edition of 250, exclusive to U.K. International Ceramics Ltd.

DB124
ROCK AND ROLL BUNNYKINS™

Designer:	Harry Sales
Modeller:	David Lyttleton
Height:	4 1/2", 11.4 cm
Colour:	White, blue and red
Issued:	1991 (© 1991)

Back	Price			
Stamp	U.S. $	Can. $	U.K. £	Aust. $
BK-Special	225.00	250.00	85.00	350.00

Note: Produced exclusively for Royal Doulton U.S.A. and the Rock and Roll Hall of Fame, Cleveland, in a limited edition of 1,000.

DB125
MILKMAN BUNNYKINS™

Designer:	Graham Tongue
Modeller:	Amanda Hughes-Lubeck
Height:	4 1/2", 11.4 cm
Colour:	White, green and grey
Issued:	1992 (© 1991)

| Back Stamp | Price | | | |
	U.S. $	Can. $	U.K. £	Aust. $
BK-Special	250.00	300.00	100.00	300.00

Note: Commissioned by U.K. International Ceramics Ltd. in a special edition of 1,000.

DB126
MAGICIAN BUNNYKINS™

Designer:	Graham Tongue
Modeller:	Warren Platt
Height:	4 1/2", 11.4 cm
Colour:	Black and yellow
Issued:	1992 (© 1992)

| Back Stamp | Price | | | |
	U.S. $	Can. $	U.K. £	Aust. $
BK-Special	175.00	225.00	85.00	300.00

Note: Commissioned by Pascoe & Co. and Charles Dombeck.

DB127
GUARDSMAN BUNNYKINS™

Designer:	Denise Andrews
Modeller:	Warren Platt
Height:	4 1/2", 11.4 cm
Colour:	Scarlet jacket, black trousers and bearskin hat
Issued:	1992 (© 1992)

| Back Stamp | Price | | | |
	U.S. $	Can. $	U.K. £	Aust. $
BK-Special	185.00	225.00	125.00	300.00

Note: Produced exclusively for U.K.I. Ceramics Ltd. in a special edition of 1,000.

DB128
CLOWN BUNNYKINS™
First Variation

Designer:	Denise Andrews
Modeller:	Warren Platt
Height:	4 1/4", 10.8 cm
Colour:	White costume with black patterned costume, red square on trousers and red ruff at neck
Issued:	1992 (© 1992)
Varieties:	DB 129

Back Stamp	Price			
	U.S. $	Can. $	U.K. £	Aust. $
BK-Special	600.00	675.00	250.00	750.00

Note: Produced exclusively for U.K.I. Ceramics Ltd. in a special edition of 750.

DB129
CLOWN BUNNYKINS™
Second Variation

Designer:	Denise Andrews
Modeller:	Warren Platt
Height:	4 1/4", 10.8 cm
Colour:	White costume with red patterned costume, black ruff around neck
Issued:	1992 (© 1992)
Varieties:	DB 128

Back Stamp	Price			
	U.S. $	Can. $	U.K. £	Aust. $
BK-Special	1,500.00	1,500.00	500.00	950.00

Note: Produced exclusively for U.K.I. Ceramics Ltd. in a special edition of 250.

DB130
SWEETHEART BUNNYKINS™

Designer:	Graham Tongue
Modeller:	Warren Platt
Height:	3 3/4", 9.5 cm
Colour:	Yellow sweater, blue trousers, red heart
Issued:	1992 to the present (© 1992)

Back Stamp	Price			
	U.S. $	Can. $	U.K. £	Aust. $
BK-5	40.00	58.50	14.95	75.00

Note: Introduced at the International Collectables Exposition at South Bend, Indiana, in July 1992.

DB131
MASTER POTTER BUNNYKINS™

Designer:	Graham Tongue
Modeller:	Warren Platt
Height:	3 3/4", 9.3 cm
Colour:	Blue, white, green and brown
Issued:	1993 - 1993 (© 1992)
Series:	R.D.I.C.C.

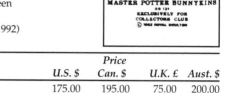

Back Stamp	Price			
	U.S. $	Can. $	U.K. £	Aust. $
BK-Special	175.00	195.00	75.00	200.00

Note: Produced exclusively for the Royal Doulton International Collectors Club in 1993.

DB132
HALLOWEEN BUNNYKINS™

Designer:	Graham Tongue
Modeller:	Martyn Alcock
Height:	3 1/4", 8.3 cm
Colour:	Orange and yellow pumpkin
Issued:	1993 to the present (© 1993)

Back Stamp	Price			
	U.S. $	Can.$	U.K. £	Aust. $
BK-5	50.00	78.50	17.95	85.00

Note: Pre-released in the U.S.A. in 1993.

DB133
AUSSIE SURFER BUNNYKINS™

Designer:	Graham Tongue
Modeller:	Martyn Alcock
Height:	4", 10.1 cm
Colour:	Gold and green outfit, white and blue base
Issued:	1994 - 1994

Back Stamp	Price			
	U.S. $	Can. $	U.K. £	Aust. $
BK-Special	125.00	150.00	75.00	95.00

Note: Produced exclusively for Royal Doulton, Australia.

DB134
JOHN BULL BUNNYKINS™

Designer:	Denise Andrews
Modeller:	Amanda Hughes-Lubeck
Height:	4 1/2", 11 cm
Colour:	Grey, yellow, red, white and blue Union Jack waistcoat
Issued:	1993 (© 1993)

Back Stamp	Price			
	U.S. $	Can. $	U.K. £	Aust. $
BK-Special	195.00	275.00	110.00	225.00

Note: Produced exclusively for U.K. International Ceramics Ltd. in a special limited edition of 1,000.

DB135
MOUNTIE BUNNYKINS™

Designer:	Graham Tongue
Modeller:	Warren Platt
Height:	4", 10.1 cm
Colour:	Red jacket, dark blue trousers and brown hat
Issued:	1993 (© 1993)

Back Stamp	Price			
	U.S. $	Can. $	U.K. £	Aust. $
BK-Special	325.00	450.00	275.00	850.00

Note: Produced exclusively for the Doulton Collectors Weekend in Toronto, September 1993, in a special edition of 750 (120th anniversary of the R.C.M.P., 1873-1993).

DB136
SERGEANT MOUNTIE BUNNYKINS™

Designer:	Graham Tongue
Modeller:	Warren Platt
Height:	4", 10.1 cm
Colour:	Red jacket, dark blue trousers, brown hat and yellow stripes
Issued:	1993 (© 1993)

Back Stamp	Price			
	U.S. $	Can. $	U.K. £	Aust. $
BK-Special	1,100.00	1,375.00	725.00	1,500.00

Note: Produced exclusively for the Doulton Collectors Weekend in Toronto, September, 1993 in a special edition of 250 (120th anniversary of the R.C.M.P., 1873-1993).

DB137
60TH ANNIVERSARY BUNNYKINS™

Designer:	Denise Andrews
Modeller:	Warren Platt
Height:	4 1/2", 11 cm
Colour:	Lemon, yellow and white
Issued:	1994 - 1994

Back Stamp	Price U.S. $	Can. $	U.K. £	Aust. $
BK-6	60.00	75.00	45.00	100.00

DB142
CHEERLEADER BUNNYKINS™
First Variation

Designer:	Denise Andrews
Modeller:	Warren Platt
Height:	4 1/2", 11 cm
Colour:	Red
Issued:	1994 - 1994

Back Stamp	Price U.S. $	Can. $	U.K. £	Aust. $
BK-Special	150.00	200.00	38.00	175.00

Note: Produced exclusively for U.K.I. Ceramics Ltd. in a special edition of 1,000.

DB143
CHEERLEADER BUNNYKINS™
Second Variation

Designer:	Denise Andrews
Modeller:	Warren Platt
Height:	4 1/2", 11 cm
Colour:	Yellow
Issued:	1994 - 1994

Back Stamp	Price U.S. $	Can. $	U.K. £	Aust. $
BK-Special	150.00	200.00	40.00	175.00

Note: Produced exclusively for U.K.I. Ceramics Ltd. in a special edition of 1,000 for Doulton Fairs in England.

DB144
BATSMAN BUNNYKINS™

Designer:	Denise Andrews
Modeller:	Amanda Hughes-Lubeck
Height:	4", 10.1 cm
Colour:	White, beige and black
Issued:	1994

Back Stamp	Price U.S. $	Can. $	U.K. £	Aust. $
BK-Special	200.00	250.00	65.00	250.00

Note: Produced exclusively for U.K.I. Ceramics Ltd. in a special edition of 1,000.

DB145
BOWLER BUNNYKINS™

Designer:	Denise Andrews
Modeller:	Warren Platt
Height:	4", 10.1 cm
Colour:	White, beige and black
Issued:	1994

Back Stamp	Price U.S. $	Can. $	U.K. £	Aust. $
BK-Special	200.00	250.00	65.00	250.00

Note: Produced exclusively for U.K.I. Ceramics Ltd. in a special edition of 1,000.

DB146
CHRISTMAS SURPRISE BUNNYKINS™

Designer:	Graham Tongue
Modeller:	Warren Platt
Height:	3 1/2", 8.9 cm
Colour:	Cream and red
Issued:	1994 to the present (©1994)

Back Stamp	Price U.S. $	Can. $	U.K. £	Aust. $
BK-6	50.00	78.50	18.95	85.00

DB147
RAINY DAY BUNNYKINS™

Designer:	Graham Tongue
Modeller:	Warren Platt
Height:	4", 10.1 cm
Colour:	Yellow coat and hat, blue trousers, black boots
Issued:	1994 to the present (© 1994)

RAINY DAY
BUNNYKINS
DB 147
© 1994 ROYAL DOULTON

Back Stamp	Price			
	U.S. $	Can. $	U.K. £	Aust. $
BK-6	40.00	58.50	14.95	75.00

DB148
BATHTIME BUNNYKINS™

Designer:	Graham Tongue
Modeller:	Warren Platt
Height:	4", 10.1 cm
Colour:	White bathrobe with grey trim, yellow towel and duck
Issued:	1994 to the present (©1994)

BATHTIME BUNNYKINS
DB 148
© 1994 ROYAL DOULTON

Back Stamp	Price			
	U.S. $	Can. $	U.K. £	Aust. $
BK-6	40.00	58.50	14.95	75.00

DB149
EASTER GREETINGS BUNNYKINS™

Designer:	Graham Tongue
Modeller:	Warren Platt
Height:	4 1/2", 11.4 cm
Colour:	Yellow, white and green
Issued:	1995 to the present (© 1994)

EASTER GREETINGS
BUNNYKINS
DB 149
© 1994 ROYAL DOULTON

Back Stamp	Price			
	U.S. $	Can. $	U.K. £	Aust. $
BK-6	50.00	74.00	17.95	85.00

DB150
WICKETKEEPER BUNNYKINS™

Designer:	Denise Andrews
Modeller:	Amanda Hughes-Lubeck
Height:	3 1/2", 8.9 cm
Colour:	White, beige and black
Issued:	1995 (©1994)

Back Stamp	Price			
	U.S. $	Can. $	U.K. £	Aust. $
BK-6 Special	175.00	300.00	125.00	250.00

Note: Produced exclusively for U.K.I. Ceramics Ltd. in a special edition of 1,000.

DB151
PARTNERS IN COLLECTING™

Designer:	Walter Hayward
Modeller:	Albert Hallam
Height:	3", 7.6 cm
Colour:	Red, white and blue
Issued:	1995 - 1995
Varieties:	Also called Storytime Bunnykins, DB9, DB59

Back Stamp	Price			
	U.S. $	Can. $	U.K. £	Aust. $
BK-6	100.00	150.00	35.00	95.00

Note: Commissioned to celebrate the 15th anniversary of the R.D.I.C.C. and sold at the club convention in Williamsburg.

DB152
BOY SKATER BUNNYKINS™

Designer:	Graham Tongue
Modeller:	Martyn Alcock
Height:	4 1/4", 10.8 cm
Colour:	Blue coat, brown pants, yellow hat, green boots and black skates
Issued:	1995 to the present

Back Stamp	Price			
	U.S. $	Can. $	U.K. £	Aust. $
BK-6	40.00	63.50	17.95	79.00

DB153
GIRL SKATER BUNNYKINS™

Designer:	Graham Tongue	
Modeller:	Martyn Alcock	
Height:	3 1/2", 8.9 cm	
Colour:	Green coat with white trim, pink dress, blue books, yellow skates	
Issued:	1995 to the present	

Back Stamp	Price			
	U.S. $	Can. $	U.K. £	Aust. $
BK-6	40.00	63.50	17.95	79.00

DB154
FATHER BUNNYKINS™

Designer:	Graham Tongue
Modeller:	Martyn Alcock
Height:	4", 10.5 cm
Colour:	Red and white striped blazer, creamy yellow trousers
Issued:	1996 - 1996
Series:	Figure of the year (Holiday Outing)

Back Stamp	Price			
	U.S. $	Can. $	U.K. £	Aust. $
BK-6	50.00	74.00	19.95	75.00

DB155
MOTHER'S DAY BUNNYKINS™

Designer:	Graham Tongue
Modeller:	Shane Ridge
Height:	3 1/2", 8.9 cm
Colour:	Brown and blue
Issued:	1995 to the present

Back Stamp	Price			
	U.S. $	Can. $	U.K. £	Aust. $
BK-6	50.00	74.00	18.95	79.00

DB156
GARDENER BUNNYKINS™

Designer:	Graham Tongue
Modeller:	Warren Platt
Height:	4 1/4", 10.8 cm
Colour:	Brown jacket, white shirt, grey trousers, light green wheelbarrow
Issued:	1996 to the present

Back Stamp	Price			
	U.S. $	Can. $	U.K. £	Aust. $
BK-6	40.00	60.00	17.95	75.00

DB157
GOODNIGHT BUNNYKINS™

Designer:	Graham Tongue
Modeller:	Shane Ridge
Height:	3 3/4", 9.5 cm
Colour:	Pink nightgown, reddish brown teddy, blue and white base
Issued:	1995 to the present

Back Stamp	Price			
	U.S. $	Can. $	U.K. £	Aust. $
BK-6	40.00	63.50	15.95	69.00

DB158
NEW BABY BUNNYKINS™

Designer:	Graham Tongue
Modeller:	Graham Tongue
Height:	3 3/4", 9.5 cm
Colour:	Blue dress with white trim, white cradle, pink pillow, yellow blanket
Issued:	1995 to the present

Back Stamp	Price			
	U.S. $	Can. $	U.K. £	Aust. $
BK-6	40.00	63.50	16.95	79.00

DB160
OUT FOR A DUCK BUNNYKINS™

Designer:	Denise Andrews
Modeller:	Amanda Hughes-Lubeck
Height:	4", 10.1 cm
Colour:	White, beige and green
Issued:	1995 (©1995)

OUT FOR A DUCK BUNNYKINS
DB 160
PRODUCED EXCLUSIVELY
FOR U.K.I. CERAMICS LTD.
IN A SPECIAL EDITION OF 1,250
© 1995 ROYAL DOULTON

Back Stamp	Price			
	U.S. $	Can. $	U.K. £	Aust. $
BK-Special	175.00	225.00	100.00	200.00

Note: Produced exclusively for U.K.I. Ceramics Ltd. in a special edition of 1,250.

DB161
JESTER BUNNYKINS™

Designer:	Denise Andrews
Modeller:	Shane Ridge
Height:	4 1/2", 11.9 cm
Colour:	Red, green and yellow
Issued:	1995 (©1995)

Back Stamp	Price			
	U.S. $	Can. $	U.K. £	Aust. $
BK-Special	325.00	375.00	150.00	200.00

Note: Produced exclusively for U.K.I. Ceramics Ltd. in a special edition of 1,500.

DB162
TRICK OR TREAT BUNNYKINS™

Designer:	Denise Andrews
Modeller:	Amanda Hughes-Lubeck
Height:	4 1/2", 11.9 cm
Colour:	Red dress, black hat, shoes and cloak, white moons and stars
Issued:	1995 (©1995)

Back Stamp	Price			
	U.S. $	Can. $	U.K. £	Aust. $
BK-Special	325.00	375.00	150.00	200.00

Note: Produced exclusively for U.K.I. Ceramics Ltd. in a special edition of 1,500.

DB164
JUGGLER BUNNYKINS™

Designer:	Denise Andrews
Modeller:	Warren Platt
Height:	4 1/2", 11.9 cm
Colour:	Blue suit, black pompons, white ruff
Issued:	1996 (©1996)

Back		Price		
Stamp	U.S. $	Can. $	U.K. £	Aust. $
BK-Special	120.00	165.00	45.00	165.00

Note: Produced exclusively for U.K.I. Ceramics Ltd. in a special edition of 1,500.

DB165
RINGMASTER BUNNYKINS™

Designer:	Denise Andrews
Modeller:	Warren Platt
Height:	4 1/2", 11.9 cm
Colour:	Black hat and trousers, red jacket, white waistcoat and shirt, black bowtie
Issued:	1996 (© 1996)

Back		Price		
Stamp	U.S. $	Can. $	U.K. £	Aust. $
BK-Special	125.00	165.00	48.00	165.00

Note: Produced exclusively for U.K.I. Ceramics Ltd. in a special edition of 1,500.

D6966A
LONDON CITY GENT
BUNNYKINS TEAPOT™

Designer:	Unknown
Modeller:	Martyn Alcock
Height:	8", 20.3 cm
Colour:	Brown and black
Issued:	1994 (© 1994)
Varieties:	D6966B
Series:	Bunnykins Teapots of the World

BUNNYKINS TEAPOTS OF THE WORLD
Hand made and hand decorated
Royal Doulton®
BUNNYKINS®
LONDON CITY GENT
D 6966
© 1994 ROYAL DOULTON
SPECIAL EDITION OF 2,500

Back		Price		
Stamp	U.S. $	Can. $	U.K. £	Aust. $
BK-Special	135.00	175.00	75.00	250.00

Note: Produced exclusively for John Sinclair, Sheffield, in a limited edition of 2,500.

D6966B
U.S.A. PRESIDENT BUNNYKINS TEAPOT™

Designer:	Unknown
Modeller:	Shane Ridge
Height:	8", 20.3 cm
Colour:	Red, white and blue
Issued:	1995 (©1995)
Varieties:	D6966A
Series:	Bunnykins Teapots of the World

Royal Doulton®
BUNNYKINS®
U.S.A. PRESIDENT
D 6996
© 1995 ROYAL DOULTON
SPECIAL EDITION OF 2,500

Back Stamp	Price			
	U.S. $	Can. $	U.K. £	Aust. $
BK-Special	150.00	185.00	65.00	200.00

Note: Produced exclusively for John Sinclair, Sheffield, in a limited edition of 2,500.

D7027
AUSSIE EXPLORER BUNNYKINS TEAPOT™

Designer:	Unknown
Modeller:	Unknown
Height:	7 3/4", 19.5 cm
Colour:	Brown bunny, yellow waistcoat, green hat, orange boomerang
Issued:	1996 (©1996)
Series:	Bunnykins Teapots of the World

Royal Doulton®
BUNNYKINS®
AUSSIE EXPLORER
D 7027
© 1996 ROYAL DOULTON
SPECIAL EDITION OF 2,500

Back Stamp	Price			
	U.S. $	Can. $	U.K. £	Aust. $
BK-Special	—	—	55.00	—

Note: Produced exclusively for John Sinclair, Sheffield, in a special edition of 2,500.

COUNTRY COUSINS

PM 2101
SWEET SUZIE
"Thank You"

Designer:	Unknown
Height:	2 3/4", 7 cm
Colour:	Brown and yellow pinafore, brown rabbit
Issued:	1994 - 1994

Back Stamp	Beswick Number	Price U.S. $	Can. $	U.K. £	Aust. $
BK-1	PM2101	30.00	40.00	18.00	40.00

PM 2102
PETER
"Once Upon A Time"

Designer:	Unknown
Height:	2 1/2", 5.6 cm
Colour:	Blue suit, white bowtie, brown pencil
Issued:	1994 - 1994

Back Stamp	Beswick Number	Price U.S. $	Can. $	U.K. £	Aust. $
BK-1	PM2102	30.00	40.00	18.00	40.00

PM 2103
HARRY
"A New Home for Fred"

Designer:	Unknown
Height:	2", 5 cm
Colour:	Blue and white striped top, brown trousers, yellow bird
Issued:	1994 - 1994

Back Stamp	Beswick Number	Price U.S. $	Can. $	U.K. £	Aust. $
BK-1	PM2103	30.00	40.00	18.00	40.00

PM 2104
MICHAEL
"Happily Ever After"

Designer: Unknown
Height: 2 1/2", 6.4 cm
Colour: Green jacket, yellow pencil,
brown rabbit
Issued: 1994 - 1994

Back Stamp	Beswick Number	U.S. $	Can. $	U.K. £	Aust. $
BK-1	PM2104	30.00	40.00	18.00	40.00

PM 2105
BERTRAM
"Ten Out of Ten"

Designer: Unknown
Height: 3", 7.6 cm
Colour: Green and blue striped waistcoat,
red bow, blue mortar board
with red tassel, brown owl
Issued: 1994 - 1994

Back Stamp	Beswick Number	U.S. $	Can. $	U.K. £	Aust. $
BK-1	PM2105	30.00	40.00	18.00	40.00

PM 2106
LEONARDO
"Practice Makes Perfect"

Designer: Unknown
Height: 2 3/4", 7 cm
Colour: Brown owl, blue paintbrush,
brown hat, white palette
Issued: 1994 - 1994

Back Stamp	Beswick Number	U.S. $	Can. $	U.K. £	Aust. $
BK-1	PM2106	30.00	40.00	18.00	40.00

PM 2107
LILY
"Flowers Picked Just for You"

Designer:	Unknown
Height:	3", 7.6 cm
Colour:	Pink dress with matching bonnet, yellow pinafore with white collar, white ribbon on bonnet, brown hedgehog
Issued:	1994 - 1994

Back Stamp	Beswick Number	U.S. $	Price Can. $	U.K. £	Aust. $
BK-1	PM2107	30.00	40.00	18.00	40.00

PM 2108
PATRICK
"This Way's Best"

Designer:	Unknown
Height:	3", 7.6 cm
Colour:	Brown owl, blue and yellow checked waistcoat, yellow hat with red band, blue bowtie, white collar
Issued:	1994 - 1994

Back Stamp	Beswick Number	U.S. $	Price Can. $	U.K. £	Aust. $
BK-1	PM2108	30.00	40.00	18.00	40.00

PM 2109
JAMIE
"Hurrying Home"

Designer:	Unknown
Height:	3", 7.6 cm
Colour:	Brown hedgehog, pink sailor top with white stripes, blue trousers
Issued:	1994 - 1994

Back Stamp	Beswick Number	U.S. $	Price Can. $	U.K. £	Aust. $
BK-1	PM2109	30.00	40.00	18.00	40.00

PM 2111
MUM AND LIZZIE
"Let's Get Busy"

Designer:	Unknown
Height:	3 1/4", 8.3 cm
Colour:	Large rabbit - brown rabbit, blue dress with white pinafore
	Small rabbit - brown rabbit, white pinafore
Issued:	1994 - 1994

Back Stamp	Beswick Number	U.S. $	Price Can. $	U.K. £	Aust. $
BK-1	PM2111	40.00	60.00	25.00	50.00

PM 2112
MOLLY AND TIMMY
"Picnic Time"

Designer:	Unknown
Height:	2 3/4", 7 cm
Colour:	Large mouse - brown mouse, pink dress, blue pinafore, yellow bonnet
	Small mouse - brown mouse, yellow dungarees, white top, blue hat, brown teddy bear
Issued:	1994 - 1994

Back Stamp	Beswick Number	U.S. $	Price Can. $	U.K. £	Aust. $
BK-1	PM2112	40.00	60.00	25.00	50.00

PM 2113
POLLY AND SARAH
"Good News!"

Designer:	Unknown
Height:	3 1/4", 8.3 cm
Colour:	Rabbit - brown, blue dress, pink apron
	Hedgehog - brown, blue dress, green jacket, white pinafore, blue scarf
Issued:	1994 - 1994

Back Stamp	Beswick Number	U.S. $	Price Can. $	U.K. £	Aust. $
BK-1	PM2113	40.00	60.00	25.00	50.00

PM 2114
BILL AND TED
"Working Together"

Designer:	Unknown
Height:	3 1/4", 8.3 cm
Colour:	Mouse - brown, blue dungarees
	Hedgehog - brown, green dungarees
Issued:	1994 - 1994

BESWICK INTERNATIONAL
COUNTRY COUSINS
BILL & TED
"Working together"
PM 2114
Made in China © 1994

Back Stamp	Beswick Number	Price U.S. $	Can. $	U.K. £	Aust. $
BK-1	PM2114	40.00	60.00	25.00	50.00

PM 2115
JACK AND DAISY
"How Does Your Garden Grow"

Designer:	Unknown
Height:	2 3/4", 7 cm
Colour:	Male - brown mouse, white shirt, blue dungarees
	Female - brown mouse, pink and white striped dress, white pinafore
Issued:	1994 - 1994

Back Stamp	Beswick Number	Price U.S. $	Can. $	U.K. £	Aust. $
BK-1	PM2115	40.00	60.00	25.00	50.00

PM 2116
ALISON AND DEBBIE
"Friendship is Fun"

Designer:	Unknown
Height:	2 3/4", 7 cm
Colour:	Rabbit - brown, pink dress, white pinafore
	Squirrel - brown, blue dress, pink apron
Issued:	1994 - 1994

Back Stamp	Beswick Number	Price U.S. $	Can. $	U.K. £	Aust. $
BK-1	PM2116	40.00	60.00	25.00	50.00

PM 2119
ROBERT AND ROSIE
"Perfect Partners"

Designer:	Unknown
Height:	3 1/4", 8.3 cm
Colour:	Male - brown squirrel, blue dungarees, blue hat with red band
	Female - brown squirrel, pink dress with white collar, yellow hat
Issued:	1994 - 1994

Back Stamp	Beswick Number	U.S. $	Price Can. $	U.K. £	Aust. $
BK-1	PM2119	40.00	60.00	25.00	50.00

PM 2120
SAMMY
"Treasure Hunting"

Designer:	Unknown
Height:	2 1/4", 5.7 cm
Colour:	Brown squirrel, green shirt, blue sack
Issued:	1994 - 1994

BESWICK INTERNATIONAL
COUNTRY COUSINS
SAMMY
"Treasure hunting"
PM 2120
Made in China © 1994

Back Stamp	Beswick Number	U.S. $	Price Can. $	U.K. £	Aust. $
BK-1	PM2120	30.00	40.00	18.00	40.00

DAVID HAND'S ANIMALAND

1148
DINKUM PLATYPUS™

Designer:	Arthur Gredington
Height:	4 1/4", 10.8 cm
Colour:	Brown and beige platypus, green base
Issued:	1949 - 1955

Beswick Number	Price			
	U.S. $	*Can. $*	*U.K. £*	*Aust. $*
1148	175.00	225.00	100.00	175.00

1150
ZIMMY LION™

Designer:	Arthur Gredington
Height:	3 3/4", 9.5 cm
Colour:	Brown lion with white face
Issued:	1949 - 1955

Beswick Number	Price			
	U.S. $	*Can. $*	*U.K. £*	*Aust. $*
1150	450.00	525.00	275.00	225.00

1151
FELIA™

Designer:	Arthur Gredington
Height:	4", 10.1 cm
Colour:	Green cat
Issued:	1949 - 1955

Beswick Number	Price			
	U.S. $	*Can. $*	*U.K. £*	*Aust. $*
1151	625.00	775.00	400.00	225.00

1152
GINGER NUTT™

Designer:	Arthur Gredington
Height:	4", 10.1 cm
Colour:	Brown and beige squirrel, green base
Issued:	1949 - 1955

| Beswick | | Price | | | |
Number			U.S. $	Can. $	U.K. £	Aust. $
1152			725.00	800.00	450.00	225.00

1153
HAZEL NUTT™

Designer:	Arthur Gredington
Height:	3 3/4", 9.5 cm
Colour:	Brown and beige squirrel, green base
Issued:	1949 - 1955

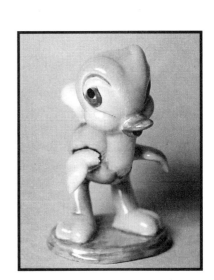

| Beswick | | Price | | | |
Number		U.S. $	Can. $	U.K. £	Aust. $
1153		725.00	800.00	450.00	225.00

1154
OSCAR OSTRICH™

Designer:	Arthur Gredington
Height:	3 3/4", 9.5 cm
Colour:	Beige and mauve, brown base
Issued:	1949 - 1955

| Beswick | | Price | | | |
Number			U.S. $	Can. $	U.K. £	Aust. $
1154			625.00	775.00	400.00	225.00

1155
DUSTY MOLE™

Designer:	Arthur Gredington
Height:	3 1/2", 8.9 cm
Colour:	Blue mole, white face
Issued:	1949 - 1955

| Beswick Number | Price | | | |
	U.S. $	Can. $	U.K. £	Aust. $
1155	300.00	375.00	175.00	225.00

1156
LOOPY HARE™

Designer:	Arthur Gredington
Height:	4 1/4", 10.8 cm
Colour:	Brown and beige hare
Issued:	1949 - 1955

| Beswick Number | Price | | | |
	U.S. $	Can. $	U.K. £	Aust. $
1156	425.00	500.00	250.00	225.00

ENGLISH COUNTRY FOLK

ECF1
HUNTSMAN FOX™

Designer:	Amanda Hughes-Lubeck
Height:	5 3/4", 14.6 cm
Colour:	Dark green jacket and cap, blue-grey trousers, green Wellingtons
Issued:	1993 to the present

ECF 1

HUNTSMAN FOX

Beswick Number		Price			
		U.S. $	Can. $	U.K. £	Aust. $
9150		64.00	80.00	23.95	99.00

ECF2
FISHERMAN OTTER™

Designer:	Warren Platt
Height:	5 3/4", 14.6 cm
Colour:	Yellow shirt and hat, dark green waistcoat, blue-grey trousers, green Wellingtons
Issued:	1993 to the present

ECF 2

FISHERMAN OTTER

Beswick Number	Price			
	U.S. $	Can. $	U.K. £	Aust. $
9152	64.00	80.00	23.95	99.00

ECF3
GARDENER RABBIT™

Designer:	Warren Platt
Height:	6", 15.0 cm
Colour:	White shirt, red pullover, blue trousers, grey hat, black Wellingtons
Issued:	1993 to the present

ECF 3

GARDENER RABBIT

Beswick Number		Price			
		U.S. $	Can. $	U.K. £	Aust. $
9155		64.00	80.00	23.95	99.00

ECF4
GENTLEMAN PIG™

Designer:	Amanda Hughes-Lubeck
Height:	5 3/4", 14.6 cm
Colour:	Brown suit
Issued:	1993 to the present

| Beswick | | Price | | |
Number	U.S. $	Can. $	U.K. £	Aust. $
9149	64.00	80.00	23.95	99.00

ECF5
SHEPHERD SHEEPDOG™

Designer:	Warren Platt
Height:	6 3/4", 17.2 cm
Colour:	Yellow smock
Issued:	1993 to the present

| Beswick | | Price | | |
Number	U.S. $	Can. $	U.K. £	Aust. $
9156	64.00	80.00	23.95	95.00

ECF6
HIKER BADGER™

Designer:	Warren Platt
Height:	5 1/4", 13.3 cm
Colour:	Yellow shirt, blue waistcoat,
	red cap and socks
Issued:	1993 to the present

| Beswick | | Price | | |
Number	U.S. $	Can. $	U.K. £	Aust. $
9157	64.00	80.00	23.95	95.00

ECF7
MRS RABBIT BAKING™

Designer:	Martyn Alcock
Height:	5 1/2", 14.0 cm
Colour:	Mauve dress, white apron and cap
Issued:	1994 to the present

ECF 7
MRS RABBIT BAKING

Beswick Number	Price U.S. $	Can. $	U.K. £	Aust. $
Unknown	64.00	90.00	23.95	95.00

ECF8
THE LADY PIG™

Designer:	Amanda Hughes-Lubeck
Height:	5 1/2", 14.0 cm
Colour:	Green jacket, skirt and hat, brown umbrella
Issued:	1995 to the present

ECF 8
THE LADY PIG

Beswick Number	Price U.S. $	Can. $	U.K. £	Aust. $
Unknown	64.00	90.00	23.95	95.00

HANNA-BARBERA

3577
PEBBLES™

Designer: Simon Ward
Height: 3 1/2", 8.9 cm
Colour: Green dress, blue pants, red hair,
light brown base
Issued: 1997

Beswick		Price		
Number	U.S. $	Can. $	U.K. £	Aust. $
3577	—	—	—	—

Note: Commissioned by U.K. International Ceramics in a limited edition of 2,000.

3583
WILMA FLINTSTONE™

Designer: Simon Ward
Height: 4 3/4", 12.1 cm
Colour: White dress, red hair, light brown base
Issued: 1996

Beswick		Price		
Number	U.S. $	Can. $	U.K. £	Aust. $
3583 (Pair with Fred)	—	—	87.50	—

Note: Commissioned by U.K. International Ceramics in a limited edition of 2,000.

3584
BETTY RUBBLE™

Designer: Simon Ward
Height: 4", 10.1 cm
Colour: Blue dress, black hair, light brown base
Issued: 1996

Beswick		Price		
Number	U.S. $	Can. $	U.K. £	Aust. $
3584	—	—	—	—

Note: Commissioned by U.K. International Ceramics in a limited edition of 2,000.

3587
BARNEY RUBBLE™

Designer:	Simon Ward
Height:	3 1/2", 8.9 cm
Colour:	Reddish brown shirt, yellow hair, light brown base
Issued:	1996

Beswick Number		U.S. $	Price Can. $	U.K. £	Aust. $
3587		—	—	—	—

Note: Commissioned by U.K. International Ceramics in a limited edition of 2,000.

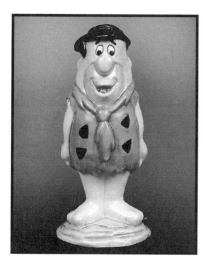

3588
FRED FLINTSTONE™

Designer:	Simon Ward
Height:	4 3/4", 12.1 cm
Colour:	Light brown shirt with dark patches, black hair, blue tie, light brown base
Issued:	1996

Beswick Number		U.S. $	Price Can. $	U.K. £	Aust. $
3588	(Pair with Wilma)	—	—	87.50	—

Note: Commissioned by U.K. International Ceramics in a limited edition of 2,000.

3590
DINO™

Designer:	Simon Ward
Height:	4 3/4", 12.1 cm
Colour:	Red, white and light brown
Issued:	1997

Beswick Number		U.S. $	Price Can. $	U.K. £	Aust. $
3590		—	—	—	—

Note: Commissioned by U.K. International Ceramics in a limited edition of 2,000.

BAMM BAMM™

Designer:	Simon Ward
Height:	3", 7.6 cm
Colour:	Light and dark brown pants, white hair, yellow club, light brown base
Issued:	1997

Beswick		Price			
Number			U.S. $	Can. $	U.K. £	Aust. $
			—	—	—	—

Note: Commissioned by U.K. International Ceramics in a limited edition of 2,000.

TOP CAT™

Designer:	Simon Ward
Height:	5", 12.7 cm
Colour:	Yellow with mauve waistcoat and hat
Issued:	1996

Beswick		Price			
Number	U.S.	Can. $	U.K. £	Aust. $
	—	—	—	—

Note: Issued in an exclusive limited edition of 2,000 for the Doulton and Beswick Fairs in England.

John Beswick
TOP CAT ™
© 1996 H-B PROD., INC
LICENSED BY CPL
© 1996 ROYAL DOULTON
EXCLUSIVE EDITION OF 2,000
FOR THE DOULTON &
BESWICK FAIRS IN ENGLAND

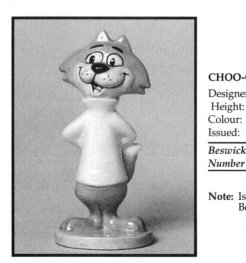

CHOO-CHOO™

Designer:	Simon Ward
Height:	4 1/2", 11.9 cm
Colour:	Pink with white shirt
Issued:	1996

John Beswick
CHOO-CHOO ™
© 1996 H-B PROD., INC.
LICENSED BY CPL
© 1996 ROYAL DOULTON
EXCLUSIVE EDITION OF 2,000
FOR THE DOULTON &
BESWICK FAIRS IN ENGLAND

Beswick		Price			
Number			U.S. $	Can. $	U.K. £	Aust. $
			—	—	—	—

Note: Issued in an exclusive limited edition of 2,000 for the Doulton and Beswick Fairs in England.

JOAN WALSH ANGLUND

2272
ANGLUND BOY™

Designer:	Albert Hallam
Height:	4 1/2", 11.9 cm
Colour:	Green dungarees, brown hat
Issued:	1969 - 1971

Beswick Number		U.S. $	Price Can. $	U.K. £	Aust. $
2272		225.00	275.00	125.00	325.00

2293
ANGLUND GIRL WITH DOLL™

Designer:	Albert Hallam
Height:	4 1/2", 11.9 cm
Colour:	Green dress and bow, white apron
Issued:	1969 - 1971

Beswick Number		U.S. $	Price Can. $	U.K. £	Aust. $
2293		225.00	275.00	125.00	325.00

2317
ANGLUND GIRL WITH FLOWERS™

Designer:	Albert Hallam
Height:	4 3/4", 12.1 cm
Colour:	White dress, blue leggings, straw hat with blue ribbon
Issued:	1969 - 1971

Beswick Number		U.S. $	Price Can. $	U.K. £	Aust. $
2317		225.00	275.00	125.00	325.00

KITTY MACBRIDE

2526
A FAMILY MOUSE™

Designer: Graham Tongue
Height: 3 1/2", 8.9 cm
Colour: Brown, mauve and turquoise, light and dark green base
Issued: 1975 - 1983

Beswick Number		Price		
	U.S. $	Can. $	U.K. £	Aust. $
2526	95.00	115.00	60.00	160.00

2527
A DOUBLE ACT™

Designer: Graham Tongue
Height: 3 1/2", 8.9 cm
Colour: Yellow, orange, brown, green and blue
Issued: 1975 - 1983

Beswick Number		Price		
	U.S. $	Can. $	U.K. £	Aust. $
2527	135.00	175.00	70.00	160.00

2528
THE RACEGOER™

Designer: David Lyttleton
Height: 3 1/2", 8.9 cm
Colour: Brown and yellow, light and dark green base
Issued: 1975 - 1983

Beswick Number		Price		
	U.S. $	Can. $	U.K. £	Aust. $
2528	85.00	100.00	40.00	160.00

2529
A GOOD READ™

Designer:	David Lyttleton
Height:	2 1/2", 6.4 cm
Colour:	Yellow, blue, brown and white
Issued:	1975 - 1983

| Beswick Number | Price | | | |
	U.S. $	Can. $	U.K. £	Aust. $
2529	475.00	575.00	250.00	325.00

2530
LAZYBONES™

Designer:	David Lyttleton
Height:	1 1/2", 3.8 cm
Colour:	Blue, black and brown, green and white base
Issued:	1975 - 1983

| Beswick Number | Price | | | |
	U.S. $	Can. $	U.K. £	Aust. $
2530	100.00	135.00	60.00	160.00

2531
A SNACK™

Designer:	David Lyttleton
Height:	3 1/4", 8.3 cm
Colour:	Brown, blue and yellow, green base
Issued:	1975 - 1983

| Beswick Number | Price | | | |
	U.S. $	Can. $	U.K. £	Aust. $
2531	85.00	110.00	45.00	160.00

2532
STRAINED RELATIONS™

Designer: David Lyttleton
Height: 3", 7.6 cm
Colour: Brown, blue and green
Issued: 1975 - 1983

Beswick		Price		
Number	U.S. $	Can. $	U.K. £	Aust. $
2532	100.00	130.00	55.00	130.00

2533
JUST GOOD FRIENDS™

Designer: David Lyttleton
Height: 3", 7.6 cm
Colour: Brown, yellow, blue, red and green
Issued: 1975 - 1983

Beswick		Price		
Number	U.S. $	Can. $	U.K. £	Aust. $
2533	150.00	185.00	75.00	180.00

2565
THE RING™

Designer: David Lyttleton
Height: 3 1/4", 8.3 cm
Colour: Brown, white, purple and yellow
Issued: 1976 - 1983

Beswick		Price		
Number	U.S. $	Can. $	U.K. £	Aust. $
2565	110.00	135.00	60.00	200.00

2566
GUILTY SWEETHEARTS™

Designer:	David Lyttleton
Height:	2 1/4", 5.7 cm
Colour:	Brown, yellow, green and white
Issued:	1976 - 1983

| Beswick | | Price | | |
Number	U.S. $	Can. $	U.K. £	Aust. $
2566	120.00	135.00	60.00	180.00

2589
ALL I DO IS THINK OF YOU™

Designer:	David Lyttleton
Height:	2 1/2", 6.4 cm
Colour:	Brown, yellow and white
Issued:	1976 - 1983

| Beswick | | Price | | |
Number	U.S. $	Can. $	U.K. £	Aust. $
2589	200.00	250.00	115.00	300.00

LITTLE LIKABLES

LL1
FAMILY GATHERING™
(Hen and Two Chicks)

Designer:	Diane Griffiths
Height:	4 1/2", 11.9 cm
Colour:	White hen and chicks with yellow beaks and gold comb on hen
Issued:	1985 - 1987

| Beswick Number | Price | | | |
	U.S. $	Can. $	U.K. £	Aust. $
LL1	50.00	70.00	35.00	80.00

LL2
WATCHING THE WORLD GO BY™
(Frog)

Designer:	Robert Tabbenor
Height:	3 3/4", 9.5 cm
Colour:	White frog, black and green eyes
Issued:	1985 - 1987

| Beswick Number | Price | | | |
	U.S. $	Can. $	U.K. £	Aust. $
LL2	90.00	110.00	60.00	100.00

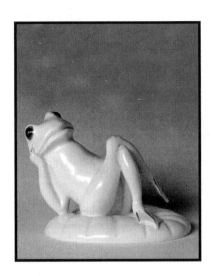

LL3
HIDE AND SEEK™
(Pig and Two Piglets)

Designer:	Robert Tabbenor
Height:	3 1/4", 8.3 cm
Colour:	White pigs with pink noses, ears and tails
Issued:	1985 - 1987

| Beswick Number | Price | | | |
	U.S. $	Can. $	U.K. £	Aust. $
LL3	50.00	70.00	35.00	80.00

LL4
MY PONY™
(Pony)

Designer:	Diane Griffiths
Height:	7 1/4", 18.4 cm
Colour:	White pony with blue highlights in mane and tail
Issued:	1985 - 1987

Beswick Number		Price		
	U.S. $	Can. $	U.K. £	Aust. $
LL4	70.00	90.00	50.00	100.00

LL5
ON TOP OF THE WORLD™
(Elephant)

Designer:	Diane Griffiths
Height:	3 3/4", 9.5 cm
Colour:	White elephant with black eyes and gold nails
Issued:	1985 - 1987

Beswick Number		Price		
	U.S. $	Can. $	U.K. £	Aust. $
LL5	50.00	70.00	35.00	80.00

LL6
TREAT ME GENTLY™
(Fawn)

Designer:	Diane Griffiths
Height:	4 1/2", 11.9 cm
Colour:	White fawn with black and brown eyes, black nose and gold hoof
Issued:	1985 - 1987

Beswick Number		Price		
	U.S. $	Can. $	U.K. £	Aust. $
LL6	50.00	70.00	35.00	80.00

LL7
OUT AT LAST™
(Duckling)

Designer:	Robert Tabbenor
Height:	3 1/4", 8.3 cm
Colour:	White duck with black and brown eyes and gold beak
Issued:	1985 - 1987

Beswick Number	Price			
	U.S. $	Can. $	U.K. £	Aust. $
LL7	50.00	70.00	35.00	80.00

LL8
CATS CHORUS™
(Cats)

Designer:	Robert Tabbenor
Height:	4 3/4", 12.1 cm
Colour:	Two white cats with black and green eyes, black nose, pink ears and mouth
Issued:	1985 - 1987

Beswick Number	Price			
	U.S. $	Can. $	U.K. £	Aust. $
LL8	50.00	70.00	35.00	80.00

LITTLE LOVABLES

LL1
HAPPY BIRTHDAY™

Designer:	Amanda Hughes-Lubeck
Height:	4 1/2", 11.9 cm
Colour:	White, pink and orange (gloss)
Issued:	1992 - 1994
Varieties:	LL8; LL15; also unnamed LL22

LL 1

Model		Price			
No.					
	U.S. $	Can. $	U.K. £	Aust. $
3328	40.00	50.00	25.00	40.00

LL2
I LOVE YOU™

Designer:	Amanda Hughes-Lubeck
Height:	4 1/2", 11.9 cm
Colour:	White, green and pink (gloss)
Issued:	1992 - 1994
Varieties:	LL9, LL16; also unnamed LL23

LL 2

Model		Price			
No.					
	U.S. $	Can. $	U.K. £	Aust. $
3320	40.00	50.00	25.00	60.00

LL3
GOD LOVES ME™

Designer:	Amanda Hughes-Lubeck
Height:	3 3/4", 9.5 cm
Colour:	White, green and turquoise (gloss)
Issued:	1992 - 1993
Varieties:	LL10, LL17; also called "Please," LL33, LL34; also unnamed LL24

Model		Price			
No.					
	U.S. $	Can. $	U.K. £	Aust. $
3336	135.00	175.00	85.00	60.00

LL4
JUST FOR YOU™

Designer: Warren Platt
Height: 4 1/2", 11.9 cm
Colour: White, pink and blue (gloss)
Issued: 1992 - 1994
Varieties: LL11, LL18; also unnamed LL25

LL 4

JUST FOR YOU

Model No.	U.S. $	Price Can. $	U.K. £	Aust. $
3361	40.00	50.00	25.00	60.00

To Mum

TO MOTHER

LL5
TO MOTHER™

Designer: Amanda Hughes-Lubeck
Height: 4 1/2", 11.9 cm
Colour: White, blue and purple (gloss)
Issued: 1992 - 1994
Varieties: LL12, LL19; also called "To Daddy,"
also unnamed LL26

LL 5

Model No.	U.S. $	Price Can. $	U.K. £	Aust. $
3331	40.00	50.00	25.00	60.00

LL6
CONGRATULATIONS™

Designer: Warren Platt
Height: 4 1/2", 11.9 cm
Colour: White, green and pink (gloss)
Issued: 1992 - 1994
Varieties: LL13, LL20; also unnamed LL27

LL 6

CONGRATULATIONS

Model No.	U.S. $	Price Can. $	U.K. £	Aust. $
3340	40.00	50.00	25.00	60.00

LL7
PASSED™

Designer:	Amanda Hughes-Lubeck
Height:	3", 7.6 cm
Colour:	White, lilac and pink (gloss)
Issued:	1992 - 1994
Varieties:	LL14, LL21; also unnamed LL28

Model No.	Price			
	U.S. $	Can. $	U.K. £	Aust. $
3334	40.00	50.00	30.00	60.00

LL8
HAPPY BIRTHDAY™

Designer:	Amanda Hughes-Lubeck
Height:	4 1/2", 11.9 cm
Colour:	White, yellow and green (gloss)
Issued:	1992 - 1994
Varieties:	LL1, LL15; also unnamed LL22

Model No.	Price			
	U.S. $	Can. $	U.K. £	Aust. $
3328	40.00	50.00	25.00	60.00

LL9
I LOVE YOU™

Designer:	Amanda Hughes-Lubeck
Height:	4 1/2", 11.9 cm
Colour:	White, blue and orange (gloss)
Issued:	1992 - 1994
Varieties:	LL2, LL16; also unnamed LL23

Model No.	Price			
	U.S. $	Can. $	U.K. £	Aust. $
3320	40.00	50.00	25.00	60.00

LL10
GOD LOVES ME™

Designer:	Amanda Hughes-Lubeck
Height:	3 3/4", 9.5 cm
Colour:	White, gold and blue (gloss)
Issued:	1992 - 1993
Varieties:	LL3, LL17; also called "Please,"
	LL33, LL34; also unnamed LL24

Model	Price			
No.	U.S. $	Can. $	U.K. £	Aust. $
3336	135.00	175.00	85.00	80.00

LL11
JUST FOR YOU™

Designer:	Warren Platt
Height:	4 1/2", 11.9 cm
Colour:	White, yellow and pale green (gloss)
Issued:	1992 - 1994
Varieties:	LL4, LL18; also unnamed LL25

Model	Price			
No.	U.S. $	Can. $	U.K. £	Aust. $
3361	40.00	50.00	25.00	60.00

LL12
TO MOTHER™

Designer:	Amanda Hughes-Lubeck
Height:	4 1/2", 11.9 cm
Colour:	White, yellow and pink (gloss)
Issued:	1992 - 1994
Varieties:	LL5, LL19; also called "To Daddy,"
	LL29; also unnamed LL26

Model	Price			
No.	U.S. $	Can. $	U.K. £	Aust. $
3331	40.00	50.00	25.00	60.00

LL13
CONGRATULATIONS™

Designer:	Warren Platt
Height:	4 1/2", 11.9 cm
Colour:	White, pale blue and yellow (gloss)
Issued:	1992 - 1994
Varieties:	LL6, LL20; also unnamed LL27

Model	Price			
No.	U.S. $	Can. $	U.K. £	Aust. $
3340	40.00	50.00	25.00	70.00

LL14
PASSED™

Designer:	Amanda Hughes-Lubeck
Height:	3", 7.6 cm
Colour:	White, light blue and orange (gloss)
Issued:	1992 - 1994
Varieties:	LL7, LL21; also unnamed LL28

Model	Price			
No.	U.S. $	Can. $	U.K. £	Aust. $
3334	40.00	50.00	30.00	60.00

LL15
HAPPY BIRTHDAY™

Designer:	Amanda Hughes-Lubeck
Height:	4 1/2", 11.9cm
Colour:	White, salmon and green (matt)
Issued:	1992 - 1993
Varieties:	LL8, LL15; also unnamed LL22

Model	Price			
No.	U.S. $	Can. $	U.K. £	Aust. $
3407	150.00	250.00	90.00	60.00

LL16
I LOVE YOU™

Designer:	Amanda Hughes-Lubeck
Height:	4 1/2", 11.9 cm
Colour:	White, green and yellow (matt)
Issued:	1992 - 1993
Varieties:	LL2, LL9; also unnamed LL23

| Model | | Price | | |
No.	U.S. $	Can. $	U.K. £	Aust. $
3406	150.00	250.00	90.00	60.00

LL17
GOD LOVES ME™

Designer:	Amanda Hughes-Lubeck
Height:	3 3/4", 9.5 cm
Colour:	White, purple and yellow (matt)
Issued:	1992 - 1993
Varieties:	LL3, LL10; also called "Please,"
	LL33, LL34; also unnamed LL24

| Model | | Price | | |
No.	U.S. $	Can. $	U.K. £	Aust.
3410	200.00	250.00	125.00	80.00

LL18
JUST FOR YOU™

Designer:	Warren Platt
Height:	4 1/2", 11.9 cm
Colour:	White, yellow and dark blue (matt)
Issued:	1992 - 1993
Varieties:	LL4, LL11; also unnamed LL25

| Model | | Price | | |
No.	U.S. $	Can. $	U.K. £	Aust. $
3412	150.00	250.00	90.00	60.00

LL19
TO MOTHER™

Designer:	Amanda Hughes-Lubeck
Height:	4 1/2", 11.9 cm
Colour:	White, green and orange (matt)
Issued:	1992 - 1993
Varieties:	LL5, LL12; also called "To Daddy," LL29; also unnamed LL26

Model No.	Price U.S. $	Can. $	U.K. £	Aust. $
3408	150.00	250.00	90.00	60.00

LL20
CONGRATULATIONS™

Designer:	Warren Platt
Height:	4 1/2", 11.9 cm
Colour:	White, blue and red (matt)
Issued:	1992 - 1993
Varieties:	LL6, LL13; also unnamed LL27

Model No.	Price U.S. $	Can. $	U.K. £	Aust. $
3411	150.00	250.00	90.00	60.00

LL21
PASSED™

Designer:	Amanda Hughes-Lubeck
Height:	3", 7.6 cm
Colour:	White, blue and orange (matt)
Issued:	1992 - 1993
Varieties:	LL7, LL14; also unnamed LL28

Model No.	Price U.S. $	Can. $	U.K. £	Aust. $
3409	150.00	250.00	100.00	60.00

LL22
(No Name)

Designer:	Unknown
Height:	4 1/2", 11.9 cm
Colour:	White, pink and orange (gloss)
Issued:	1993 - 1993
Varieties:	Also called "Happy Birthday," LL1, LL8, LL15

Model		Price			
No.					
	U.S. $	Can. $	U.K. £	Aust. $
3329	100.00	125.00	65.00	60.00

LL23
(No Name)

Designer:	Amanda Hughes-Lubeck
Height:	4 1/2", 11.9 cm
Colour:	White, green and pink (gloss)
Issued:	1993 - 1993
Varieties:	Also called "I Love You," LL2, LL9, LL16

Model		Price			
No.		U.S. $	Can. $	U.K. £	Aust. $
3320		100.00	125.00	65.00	60.00

LL24
(No Name)

Designer:	Amanda Hughes-Lubeck
Height:	3 3/4", 9.5 cm
Colour:	White, green and turquoise (gloss)
Issued:	1993 - 1993
Varieties:	Also called "God Loves Me," LL3, LL10, LL17; also called "Please," LL33, LL34

Model		Price			
No.					
	U.S. $	Can. $	U.K. £	Aust. $
3336	125.00	175.00	100.00	60.00

LL25
(No Name)

Designer: Warren Platt
Height: 4 1/2", 11.9 cm
Colour: White, pink and blue (gloss)
Issued: 1993 - 1993
Varieties: Also called "Just For You," LL4, LL11, LL18

Model No.	Price U.S. $	Can. $	U.K. £	Aust. $
3361	100.00	125.00	65.00	60.00

LL26
(No Name)

Designer: Amanda Hughes-Lubeck
Height: 4 1/4", 10.8 cm
Colour: White, blue and purple (gloss)
Issued: 1993 - 1993
Varieties: Also called "To Mother," LL5, LL12, LL19;
also called "To Daddy," LL29

Model No.	Price U.S. $	Can. $	U.K. £	Aust. $
3331	100.00	125.00	65.00	60.00

LL27
(No Name)

Designer: Warren Platt
Height: 4 1/2", 11.9 cm
Colour: White, green and pink (gloss)
Issued: 1993 - 1993
Varieties: Also called "Congratulations," LL6, LL13, LL20

Model No.	Price U.S. $	Can. $	U.K. £	Aust. $
3340	100.00	125.00	65.00	60.00

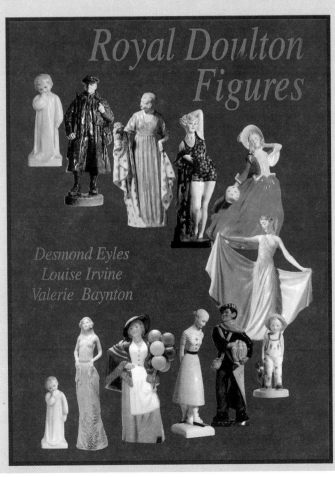

LL28
(No Name)

Designer:	Amanda Hughes-Lubeck
Height:	3", 7.6 cm
Colour:	White, lilac and pink (gloss)
Issued:	1993 - 1993
Varieties:	Also called "Passed," LL7, LL14, LL21

Model	Price			
No.	U.S. $	Can. $	U.K. £	Aust. $
3334	100.00	125.00	75.00	60.00

LL29
TO DADDY™

Designer:	Amanda Hughes-Lubeck
Height:	4 1/2", 11.9 cm
Colour:	White, light blue and green (gloss)
Issued:	1994 - 1994
Varieties:	Also called "To Mother," LL5, LL12, LL19; also unnamed LL26

Model	Price			
No.	U.S. $	Can. $	U.K. £	Aust. $
3331	60.00	75.00	40.00	60.00

LL30
MERRY CHRISTMAS™

Designer:	Amanda Hughes-Lubeck
Height:	4", 10.1 cm
Colour:	White, red and green (gloss)
Issued:	1993 - 1994

BESWICK
B
ENGLAND
LL 30

Model	Price			
No.	U.S. $	Can. $	U.K. £	Aust. $
3389	60.00	75.00	35.00	60.00

LL31
GOOD LUCK™

Designer:	Amanda Hughes-Lubeck
Height:	4 1/4", 10.8 cm
Colour:	White, pink and green (gloss)
Issued:	1993 - 1994

Model No.	Price			
	U.S. $	Can. $	U.K. £	Aust. $
3388	60.00	75.00	35.00	60.00

LL32
GET WELL SOON™

Designer:	Amanda Hughes-Lubeck
Height:	4 1/4", 10.8 cm
Colour:	White, green and purple (gloss)
Issued:	1994 - 1994

Model No.	Price			
	U.S. $	Can. $	U.K. £	Aust. $
3390	60.00	75.00	40.00	60.00

LL33
PLEASE™

Designer:	Amanda Hughes-Lubeck
Height:	3 3/4", 9.5 cm
Colour:	White, green and blue (gloss)
Issued:	1993 - 1994
Varieties:	LL34; also called "God Loves Me," LL3, LL10, LL17; also unnamed LL24

Model No.	Price			
	U.S. $	Can. $	U.K. £	Aust. $
3336	60.00	75.00	35.00	60.00

LL34
PLEASE™

Designer:	Amanda Hughes-Lubeck
Height:	3 3/4", 9.5 cm
Colour:	White, gold and light blue (gloss)
Issued:	1993 - 1994
Varieties:	LL33; also called "God Loves Me," LL3, LL10, LL17; also unnamed LL24

Model No.		U.S. $	Price Can. $	U.K. £	Aust. $
3336		60.00	75.00	35.00	60.00

Note: LL35 is the prototype for "I Love Beswick." Colourway not issued.

LL36
I LOVE BESWICK™

Designer:	Amanda Hughes-Lubeck
Height:	4 1/2", 11.9 cm
Colour:	White, green and yellow (gloss)
Issued:	1995 - 1995

Model No.		U.S. $	Price Can. $	U.K. £	Aust. $
3320		225.00	275.00	150.00	150.00

Note: This piece was specially commissioned for the Beswick Collectors Circle.

PADDINGTON BEAR CO. LTD.

PB1
PADDINGTON™
"AT THE STATION"

Designer:	Unknown
Height:	4 1/4", 11 cm
Colour:	Brown bear, blue coat, yellow hat, brown cobbled base
Issued:	1996 to the present

Royal Doulton
Paddington ™
"At the Station"
PB1
© Paddington & Co. Ltd. 1996
Licensed by ©OPYRIGHTS

Doulton Number		Price		
	U.S. $	Can. $	U.K. £	Aust. $
PB1	—	—	12.95	—

Note: This set is exclusive to the U.K.

PB2
PADDINGTON™
"BAKES A CAKE"

Designer:	Unknown
Height:	4 1/4", 11 cm
Colour:	Red jacket, black hat, multi-coloured cake, blue and white striped bowl
Issued:	1996 to the present

Royal Doulton
Paddington ™
"Bakes a Cake"
PB2
© Paddington & Co. Ltd. 1996
Licensed by ©OPYRIGHTS

Doulton Number		Price		
	U.S. $	Can. $	U.K. £	Aust. $
PB2	—	—	12.95	—

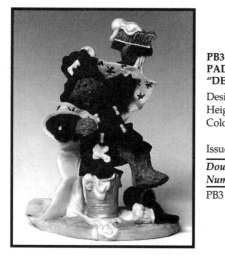

PB3
PADDINGTON™
"DECORATING"

Designer:	Unknown
Height:	4 3/4", 12 cm
Colour:	Blue coat, red hat, silver bucket, cream paint
Issued:	1996 to the present

Royal Doulton
Paddington ™
"Decorating"
PB3
© Paddington & Co. Ltd. 1996
Licensed by ©OPYRIGHTS

Doulton Number		Price		
	U.S. $	Can. $	U.K. £	Aust. $
PB3	—	—	12.95	—

PB4
PADDINGTON™
"SURFING"

Designer:	Unknown
Height:	4", 10 cm
Colour:	Multi-coloured shorts, blue hat, yellow surfboard, red rubber ring, brown suitcase
Issued:	1996 to the present

Doulton		Price			
Number	U.S. $	Can. $	U.K. £	Aust. $
PB4	—	—	12.95	—

PB5
PADDINGTON™
"GARDENING"

Designer:	Unknown
Height:	4", 10 cm
Colour:	Blue jacket, red hat, green watering can, yellow and red bucket and spade
Issued:	1996 to the present

Doulton		Price			
Number	U.S. $	Can. $	U.K. £	Aust. $
PB5	—	—	12.95	—

PB6
PADDINGTON™
"BATHTIME"

Designer:	Unknown
Height:	3 1/4", 8.5 cm
Colour:	Blue coat, yellow hat, brown scrubbing brush, yellow duck, pink soap
Issued:	1996 to the present

Doulton		Price			
Number	U.S. $	Can. $	U.K. £	Aust. $
PB6	—	—	12.95	—

PB7
PADDINGTON™
"THE GOLFER"

Designer:	Unknown
Height:	3 3/4", 9.5 cm
Colour:	White top, red and yellow sweater, red hat, green trousers, white shoes
Issued:	1996 to the present

Royal Doulton
Paddington ™
"The Golfer"
PB7
© Paddington & Co. Ltd. 1996
Licensed by ©OPYRIGHTS

Doulton Number		Price			
	U.S. $	Can. $		U.K. £	Aust. $
PB7	—	—		12.95	—

PB8
PADDINGTON™
"THE MUSICIAN"

Designer:	Unknown
Height:	3 3/4", 9.5 cm
Colour:	Black jacket, red waistcoat, brown trousers, brown violin, brass trumpet
Issued:	1996 to the present

Royal Doulton
Paddington ™
"The Musician"
PB8
© Paddington & Co. Ltd. 1996
Licensed by ©OPYRIGHTS

Doulton Number		Price			
	U.S. $	Can. $		U.K. £	Aust. $
PB8	—	—		12.95	—

PB9
PADDINGTON™
"AT CHRISTMAS TIME"

Designer:	Unknown
Height:	3 1/2", 9 cm
Colour:	Red coat, blue boots, yellow sleigh
Issued:	1996 to the present

Royal Doulton
Paddington ™
"At Christmas Time"
PB9
© Paddington & Co. Ltd. 1996
Licensed by ©OPYRIGHTS

Doulton		Price			
	U.S. $	Can. $		U.K. £	Aust. $
PB9	—	—		12.95	—

THE PIG PROMENADE

PP1
JOHN THE CONDUCTOR™
(Vietnamese Pot Bellied Pig)

Designer: Martyn Alcock
Height: 4 3/4", 12.1 cm
Colour: Black jacket, black bowtie
Issued: 1993 - 1996

Back Stamp	U.S. $	Price Can. $	U.K. £	Aust. $
PP1	66.00	90.00	29.95	99.00

PP2
MATTHEW THE TRUMPET PLAYER™
(Large White Pig)

Designer: Amanda Hughes-Lubeck
Height: 5", 12.7 cm
Colour: Light red waistcoat, black bowtie
Issued: 1993 - 1996

Back Stamp	U.S. $	Price Can. $	U.K. £	Aust. $
PP2	66.00	90.00	29.95	99.00

PP3
DAVID THE FLUTE PLAYER™
(Tamworth Pig)

Designer: Amanda Hughes-Lubeck
Height: 5 1/4", 13.3 cm
Colour: Dark green waistcoat, black bowtie
Issued: 1993 - 1996

Back Stamp	U.S. $	Price Can. $	U.K. £	Aust. $
PP3	66.00	90.00	29.95	99.00

PP4
ANDREW THE CYMBAL PLAYER™
(Gloucester Old Spotted Pig)

Designer:	Martyn Alcock
Height:	4 3/4", 12.1 cm
Colour:	Blue waistcoat, yellow cymbals,
	black bowtie
Issued:	1993 - 1996
Varieties:	Also called "George," PP10

Beswick Ware
ANDREW
PP 4

Back Stamp	Price			
	U.S. $	Can. $	U.K. £	Aust. $
PP4	66.00	90.00	29.95	99.00

PP5
DANIEL THE VIOLINIST™
(Saddleback Pig)

Designer:	Amanda Hughes-Lubeck
Height:	5 1/4", 13.3 cm
Colour:	Pale blue waistcoat, brown violin
Issued:	1993 - 1996

Beswick Ware
DANIEL
PP 5

Back Stamp	Price			
	U.S. $	Can. $	U.K. £	Aust. $
PP5	66.00	90.00	29.95	99.00

PP6
MICHAEL THE BASS DRUM PLAYER™
(Large Black Pig)

Designer:	Martyn Alcock
Height:	4 3/4", 12.1 cm
Colour:	Yellow waistcoat, red and white drum
Issued:	1993 - 1996

Beswick Ware
MICHAEL
PP 6

Back Stamp	Price			
	U.S. $	Can. $	U.K. £	Aust. $
PP6	66.00	90.00	29.95	99.00

PP7
JAMES THE TRIANGLE PLAYER™
(Tamworth Piglet)

Designer:	Warren Platt
Height:	4", 10.1 cm
Colour:	Tan, purple waistcoat; black bowtie
Issued:	1995 - 1996

Back		Price		
Stamp	U.S. $	Can. $	U.K. £	Aust. $
PP7	66.00	90.00	27.50	99.00

PP8
RICHARD THE FRENCH HORN PLAYER™

Designer:	Unknown
Height:	5 1/2", 13.3 cm
Colour:	Pale pink with dark grey spots, tan and beige waistcoat
Issued:	1996 - 1996

Back			Price	
Stamp	U.S. $	Can. $	U.K. £	Aust. $
PP8	66.00	106.00	29.95	115.00

PP9
CHRISTOPHER THE GUITAR PLAYER™

Designer:	Unknown
Height:	5 1/2", 13.3 cm
Colour:	Dark grey, yellow and cream waistcoat, black bowtie
Issued:	1996 - 1996

Back			Price	
Stamp	U.S.$	Can. $	U.K. £	Aust. $
PP9	66.00	106.00	29.95	115.00

PP10
GEORGE™

Designer:	Martyn Alcock
Height:	4 3/4", 12.1 cm
Colour:	Dark green waistcoat, yellow cymbals, black bowtie
Issued:	1996
Varieties:	Also called "Andrew," PP4

Back Stamp	U.S.$	Can. $	Price U.K. £	Aust. $
PP10	—	—	29.95	75.00

Note: Issued in a limited edition of 2,000, exclusive to John Sinclair, Sheffield.

RUPERT BEAR

2694
RUPERT BEAR™

Designer: Harry Sales
Height: 4 1/4", 10.8 cm
Colour: Red sweater, yellow check
trousers and scarf
Issued: 1980 - 1986

Beswick		Price		
Number	U.S. $	Can. $	U.K. £	Aust. $
2694	400.00	475.00	250.00	400.00

2710
ALGY PUG™

Designer: Harry Sales
Height: 4", 10.1 cm
Colour: Grey jacket, yellow waistcoat,
brown trousers
Issued: 1981 - 1986

Beswick		Price		
Number	U.S. $	Can. $	U.K. £	Aust. $
2710	165.00	195.00	100.00	175.00

2711
PONG PING™

Designer: Harry Sales
Height: 4 1/4", 10.8
Colour: Dark green jacket, gold trousers
Issued: 1981 - 1986

Beswick		Price		
Number	U.S. $	Can. $	U.K. £	Aust. $
2711	165.00	195.00	100.00	175.00

2720
BILL BADGER™

Designer:	Harry Sales
Height:	2 3/4", 7.0 cm
Colour:	Dark grey jacket, light grey trousers and red bowtie
Issued:	1981 - 1986

Beswick Number		Price		
	U.S. $	Can. $	U.K. £	Aust. $
2720	165.00	195.00	100.00	175.00

2779
RUPERT BEAR SNOWBALLING™

Designer:	Harry Sales
Height:	4 1/4", 10.8 cm
Colour:	Red coat, yellow with brown striped trousers and scarf
Issued:	1982 - 1986

Beswick Number		Price		
	U.S. $	Can. $	U.K. £	Aust. $
2779	400.00	475.00	250.00	450.00

THE SNOWMAN
GIFT COLLECTION

DS 1
JAMES™

Designer:	Harry Sales
Modeller:	David Lyttleton
Height:	3 3/4", 9.5 cm
Colour:	Blue and white striped pyjamas, brown dressing gown
Issued:	1985 - 1993
	(© 1985 R.D. [U.K.] © S ENT 1985)

Back Stamp	Price			
	U.S. $	Can. $	U.K. £	Aust. $
DS-1	150.00	225.00	80.00	110.00

DS 2
THE SNOWMAN™

Designer:	Harry Sales
Modeller:	David Lyttleton
Height:	5", 12.7 cm
Colour:	Green hat and scarf
Issued:	1985 - 1994
	(©1985 R.D. [U.K.] © S ENT 1985)

Back Stamp	Price			
	U.S. $	Can. $	U.K. £	Aust. $
DS-1	95.00	125.00	50.00	195.00

DS 3
STYLISH SNOWMAN™

Designer:	Harry Sales
Modeller:	David Lyttleton
Height:	5", 12.7 cm
Colour:	Blue trousers, lilac braces, grey hat, yellow tie with red stripes
Issued:	1985 - 1993
	(© 1985 R.D. [U.K.] © S ENT 1985)

Back Stamp	Price			
	U.S. $	Can. $	U.K. £	Aust. $
DS-1	275.00	400.00	145.00	210.00

DS 4
THANK YOU SNOWMAN™

Designer:	Harry Sales
Modeller:	David Lyttleton
Height:	5", 12.7 cm
Colour:	Snowman—green hat and scarf
	James—brown dressing gown
Issued:	1985 - 1994
	(© 1985 R.D. [U.K.] © S ENT 1985)

| Back | | Price | | |
Stamp	U.S. $	Can. $	U.K. £	Aust. $
DS-1	175.00	200.00	70.00	195.00

DS 5
SNOWMAN MAGIC MUSIC BOX™

Designer:	Harry Sales
Modeller:	David Lyttleton
Height:	8", 20.3 cm
Colour:	Cream music box with blue,
	green and pink balloon design
Issued:	1985 - 1994
	(© 1985 R.D. [U.K.] © S ENT 1985)
Tune:	"Walking in the Air"

| Back | | Price | | |
Stamp	U.S. $	Can. $	U.K. £	Aust. $
DS-1	200.00	250.00	110.00	195.00

DS 6
COWBOY SNOWMAN™

Designer:	Harry Sales
Modeller:	David Lyttleton
Height:	5", 12.7 cm
Colour:	Brown hat and holster belt
Issued:	1986 - 1992
	(© 1985 R.D. [U.K.] © S ENT 1985)

| Back | | Price | | |
Stamp	U.S. $	Can. $	U.K. £	Aust. $
DS-1	350.00	450.00	200.00	195.00

DS 7
HIGHLAND SNOWMAN™

Designer: Harry Sales
Modeller: David Lyttleton
Height: 5 1/4", 13.3 cm
Colour: Red, blue and white kilt
Issued: 1987 - 1993
(© 1985 R.D. [U.K.] © S ENT 1985)

| Doulton Number | | Price | | |
	U.S. $	Can. $	U.K. £	Aust. $
DS-1	250.00	325.00	150.00	195.00

DS 8
LADY SNOWMAN™

Designer: Harry Sales
Modeller: David Lyttleton
Height: 5", 12.7 cm
Colour: Pink apron, blue hat
Issued: 1987 - 1992
(© 1985 R.D. [U.K.] © S ENT 1985)

| Back Stamp | | Price | | |
	U.S. $	Can. $	U.K. £	Aust. $
DS-1	350.00	475.00	225.00	195.00

DS 9
BASS DRUMMER SNOWMAN™

Designer: Graham Tongue
Modeller: Warren Platt
Height: 5 1/2", 13.3 cm
Colour: Pink and yellow drum, brown straps, pale blue hat
Issued: 1987 - 1993
(© 1987 R.D. © S ENT 1987)

| Back Stamp | | Price | | |
	U.S. $	Can. $	U.K. £	Aust. $
DS-1	250.00	400.00	150.00	195.00

DS 10
FLAUTIST SNOWMAN™

Designer:	Graham Tongue
Modeller:	Warren Platt
Height:	5 1/2", 14.0 cm
Colour:	Yellow and red cap, brown tie
Issued:	1987 - 1993
	(© 1987 R.D. © S ENT 1987)

Back Stamp	Price			
	U.S. $	Can. $	U.K. £	Aust. $
DS-1	200.00	325.00	150.00	195.00

DS 11
VIOLINIST SNOWMAN™

Designer:	Graham Tongue
Modeller:	Warren Platt
Height:	5 1/4", 13.3 cm
Colour:	Green waistcoat with yellow collar, brown cap and violin, blue bowtie
Issued:	1987 - 1994
	(© 1988 R.D. © S ENT 1988)

Back Stamp	Price			
	U.S. $	Can. $	U.K. £	Aust. $
DS-1	95.00	135.00	50.00	195.00

DS 12
PIANIST SNOWMAN™

Designer:	Graham Tongue
Modeller:	Warren Platt
Height:	5", 12.7 cm
Colour:	Blue crown, orange tie
Issued:	1987 - 1994
	(© 1987 R.D. © S ENT 1987)

Back Stamp	Price			
	U.S. $	Can. $	U.K. £	Aust. $
DS-1	95.00	135.00	50.00	190.00

DS 13
SNOWMAN'S PIANO™

Designer:	Graham Tongue
Modeller:	Warren Platt
Height:	5", 13.3 cm
Colour:	White
Issued:	1987 - 1994
	(© 1987 R.D. © S ENT 1987)

Royal Doulton
THE SNOWMAN™
GIFT COLLECTION
SNOWMAN'S PIANO
DS 13
© 1987 ROYAL DOULTON
© S ENT 1987

Back Stamp	Price			
	U.S. $	Can. $	U.K. £	Aust. $
DS-1	80.00	135.00	25.00	135.00

DS 14
CYMBAL PLAYER SNOWMAN™

Designer:	Graham Tongue
Modeller:	Warren Platt
Height:	5 1/4", 13.3 cm
Colour:	Brown waistcoat, green cap and bowtie, yellow cymbals
Issued:	1988 - 1993
	(© 1988 R.D. © S ENT 1988)

Royal Doulton
THE SNOWMAN™
GIFT COLLECTION
CYMBAL PLAYER SNOWMAN
DS 14
© 1988 ROYAL DOULTON
© S ENT 1988

Back Stamp	Price			
	U.S. $	Can. $	U.K. £	Aust. $
DS-1	275.00	400.00	150.00	165.00

DS 15
DRUMMER SNOWMAN™

Designer:	Graham Tongue
Modeller:	Warren Platt
Height:	5 3/4", 14.6 cm
Colour:	Red and black hat, purple bowtie, pink and yellow drum
Issued:	1988 - 1994
	(© 1988 R.D. © S ENT 1988)

Royal Doulton
THE SNOWMAN™
GIFT COLLECTION
DRUMMER SNOWMAN
DS 15
© 1988 ROYAL DOULTON
© S ENT 1988

Back Stamp	Price			
	U.S. $	Can. $	U.K. £	Aust. $
DS-1	125.00	135.00	45.00	165.00

DS 16
TRUMPETER SNOWMAN™

Designer:	Graham Tongue
Modeller:	Warren Platt
Height:	5", 12.7 cm
Colour:	Pink hat, yellow trumpet
Issued:	1988 - 1993
	(© 1988 R.D. © S ENT 1988)

Back Stamp	Price			
	U.S. $	Can. $	U.K. £	Aust. $
DS-1	200.00	325.00	145.00	165.00

DS 17
CELLIST SNOWMAN™

Designer:	Graham Tongue
Modeller:	Warren Platt
Height:	5 1/4", 13.3 cm
Colour:	Green waistcoat with yellow collar, brown coat and cello, blue bowtie
Issued:	1988 - 1993
	(© 1985 R.D. © S ENT 1985)

Back Stamp	Price			
	U.S. $	Can. $	U.K. £	Aust. $
DS-1	95.00	150.00	45.00	165.00

DS 18
SNOWMAN MUSICAL BOX™

Designer:	Unknown
Height:	8", 22.5 cm
Colour:	Unknown
Issued:	1988 - 1990
Tune:	"Blue Bells of Scotland"

Back Sstamp	Price			
	U.S. $	Can. $	U.K. £	Aust. $
DS-1	175.00	250.00	90.00	165.00

Photograph not available at press time

DS 19
SNOWMAN MONEY BOX™

Designer:	Graham Tongue
Modeller:	Warren Platt
Height:	8 1/2", 21.6 cm
Colour:	Green hat and scarf with grey band
Issued:	1990 - 1994
	(© 1990 R.D. © S ENT 1990)

Back Stamp	Price			
	U.S. $	Can. $	U.K. £	Aust. $
DS-1	225.00	250.00	80.00	135.00

DS 20
THE SNOWMAN TOBOGGANING™

Designer:	Graham Tongue
Modeller:	Warren Platt
Height:	5", 12.7 cm
Colour:	Green hat and scarf, rose-pink toboggan
Issued:	1990 - 1994
	(© 1990 R.D. © S ENT 1990)

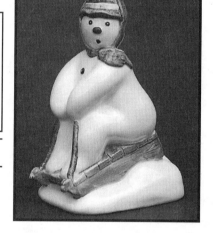

Back Stamp	Price			
	U.S. $	Can. $	U.K. £	Aust. $
DS-1	175.00	250.00	50.00	255.00

DS 21
THE SNOWMAN SKIING™

Designer:	Graham Tongue
Modeller:	Warren Platt
Height:	5", 12.7 cm
Colour:	Green hat and scarf, yellow and black goggles
Issued:	1990 - 1992
	(© 1990 R.D. © S ENT 1990)

Back Stamp	Price			
	U.S. $	Can. $	U.K. £	Aust. $
DS-1	775.00	1,000.00	600.00	175.00

DS 22
THE SNOWBALLING SNOWMAN™

Designer:	Graham Tongue
Modeller:	Warren Platt
Height:	5", 12.7 cm
Colour:	Green hat and scarf, brown tree stump
Issued:	1990 - 1994
	(© 1990 R.D. © S ENT 1990)

Back Stamp	Price U.S. $	Can. $	U.K. £	Aust. $
DS-1	125.00	225.00	50.00	175.00

DS 23
BUILDING THE SNOWMAN™

Designer:	Graham Tongue
Modeller:	Warren Platt
Height:	4", 10.1 cm
Colour:	Green hat and scarf
Issued:	1990 - 1994
	(© 1990 R.D. © S. ENT 1990)

Royal Doulton®
THE SNOWMAN™
GIFT COLLECTION
BUILDING THE
SNOWMAN
DS 23
© 1990 ROYAL DOULTON
© S. ENT 1990

Back Stamp	Price U.S. $	Can. $	U.K. £	Aust.
DS-1	150.00	200.00	50.00	110.00

D6972
SNOWMAN MINIATURE CHARACTER JUG™

Designer:	Graham Tongue
Modeller:	Martyn Alcock
Height:	2 3/4", 7.0 cm
Colour:	White, black and green
Issued:	1994 to the present

Back Stamp	Price U.S. $	Can. $	U.K. £	Aust. $
DS-1	62.00	—	50.00	110.00

Note: U.S.A. exclusive.

NORMAN THELWELL

2704A
AN ANGEL ON HORSEBACK™
First Variation

Designer: Harry Sales
Modeller: David Lyttleton
Height: 4 1/2", 11.9 cm
Colour: Grey horse, rider wears brown
           jumper, yellow pants
Issued: 1981 - 1989
Varieties: 2704B

| Beswick | Price | | | |
Number	U.S. $	Can. $	U.K. £	Aust. $
2704A	200.00	275.00	95.00	160.00

2704B
AN ANGEL ON HORSEBACK™
Second Variation

Designer: Harry Sales
Modeller: David Lyttleton
Height: 4 1/2", 11.9 cm
Colour: Bay horse, rider wears
           red jumper, yellow pants
Issued: 1981 - 1989
Varieties: 2704A

| Beswick | Price | | | |
Number	U.S. $	Can. $	U.K. £	Aust. $
2704B	175.00	250.00	80.00	145.00

2769A
KICK-START™
First Variation

Designer: Harry Sales
Modeller: David Lyttleton
Height: 3 1/2", 8.9 cm
Colour: Grey horse, rider wears
           red jersey and yellow
           pants
Issued: 1982 - 1989
Varieties: 2769B

© Norman Thelwell 1982
"Kick-Start"
John Beswick
ENGLAND

| Beswick | Price | | | |
Number	U.S. $	Can. $	U.K. £	Aust. $
2769A	200.00	275.00	85.00	165.00

2769B
KICK-START™
Second Variation

Designer:	Harry Sales
Modeller:	David Lyttleton
Height:	3 1/2", 8.9 cm
Colour:	Bay horse, rider wears red jersey and yellow pants
Issued:	1982 - 1989
Varieties:	2769B

Beswick Number	Price			
	U.S. $	Can. $	U.K. £	Aust. $
2769B	175.00	250.00	70.00	165.00

2789A
PONY EXPRESS™
First Variation

Designer:	Harry Sales
Modeller:	David Lyttleton
Height:	4 1/2", 11.9 cm
Colour:	Grey horse, rider wears green jersey and yellow trousers
Issued:	1982 - 1989
Varieties:	2789B

Beswick Number	Price			
	U.S. $	Can. $	U.K. £	Aust. $
2789A	200.00	275.00	90.00	165.00

2789B
PONY EXPRESS™
Second Variation

Designer:	Harry Sales
Modeller:	David Lyttleton
Height:	4 1/2", 11.9 cm
Colour:	Bay horse, rider wears red jersey and yellow pants
Issued:	1982 - 1989
Varieties:	2789A

Beswick Number	Price			
	U.S. $	Can. $	U.K. £	Aust. $
2789B	175.00	250.00	75.00	165.00

SS7 A
I FORGIVE YOU™
First Variation

Designer:	Harry Sales
Modeller:	David Lyttleton
Height:	4", 10.1 cm
Colour:	Grey horse, rider wears red jacket and yellow pants
Issued:	1985 - 1985
Series:	Studio Sculptures
Varieties:	SS7 B

Beswick Number	Price			
	U.S. $	Can. $	U.K. £	Aust. $
SS7A	200.00	300.00	125.00	225.00

SS7 B
I FORGIVE YOU™
Second Variation

Designer:	Harry Sales
Modeller:	David Lyttleton
Height:	4", 10.1 cm
Colour:	Bay horse, rider wears red jacket and yellow pants
Issued:	1985 - 1985
Series:	Studio Sculptures
Varieties:	SS7 A

Beswick Number	Price			
	U.S. $	Can. $	U.K. £	Aust. $
SS7B	175.00	275.00	100.00	225.00

SS12 A
EARLY BATH™
First Variation

Designer:	Harry Sales
Modeller:	David Lyttleton
Height:	4 3/4", 12.1 cm
Colour:	Grey horse, rider wears red jacket and yellow pants
Issued:	1985 - 1985
Series:	Studio Sculptures
Varieties:	SS12 A

Beswick Number	Price			
	U.S. $	Can. $	U.K. £	Aust. $
SS12A	200.00	275.00	140.00	225.00

SS12 B
EARLY BATH™
Second Variation

Designer:	Harry Sales
Height:	4 3/4", 12.1 cm
Colour:	Bay horse, rider wears red jacket and yellow pants
Issued:	1985 - 1985
Series:	Studio Sculptures
Varieties:	SS12 A

Beswick Number	U.S. $	Price Can. $	U.K. £	Aust. $
SS12B	175.00	250.00	125.00	225.00

Photograph not available at press time

THUNDERBIRDS

3337
LADY PENELOPE™

Designer:	William K. Harper
Height:	4", 10.1 cm
Colour:	Pink hat and coat, blonde hair
Issued:	1992 in a limited edition of 2,500

Beswick Number	Price			
	U.S. $	Can. $	U.K. £	Aust. $
3337		£450.00 for complete set		

3339
BRAINS™

Designer:	William K. Harper
Height:	4", 10.1 cm
Colour:	Black and blue uniform, blue glasses, black hair
Issued:	1992 in a limited edition of 2,500

Beswick Number	Price			
	U.S. $	Can. $	U.K. £	Aust. $
3339		£450.00 for complete set		

3344
SCOTT TRACY™

Designer:	William K. Harper
Height:	4", 10.1 cm
Colour:	Blue uniform, light blue band
Issued:	1992 in a limited edition of 2,500

Beswick Number	Price			
	U.S. $	Can. $	U.K. £	Aust. $
3344		£450.00 for complete set		

3345
VIRGIL TRACY™

Designer:	William K. Harper
Height:	4", 10.1 cm
Colour:	Blue uniform, yellow band
Issued:	1992 in a limited edition of 2,500

Beswick	Price			
Number	U.S. $	Can. $	U.K. £	Aust. $
3345		£450.00 for complete set		

3346
PARKER™

Designer:	William K. Harper
Height:	4", 10.1 cm
Colour:	Blue-grey uniform
Issued:	1992 in a limited edition of 2,500

Beswick	Price			
Number	U.S. $	Can. $	U.K. £	Aust. $
3346		£450.00 for complete set		

3348
THE HOOD™

Designer:	William K. Harper
Height:	4", 10.1 cm
Colour:	Browns
Issued:	1992 in a limited edition of 2,500

Beswick	Price			
Number	U.S. $	Can. $	U.K. £	Aust. $
3348		£450.00 for complete set		

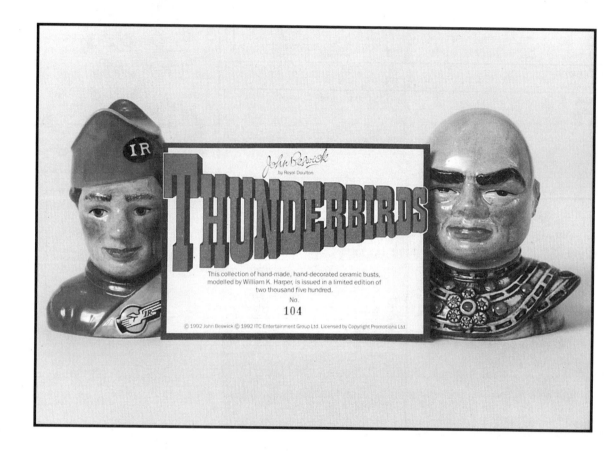

TURNER ENTERTAINMENT

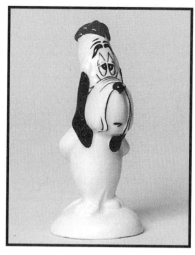

3547
DROOPY™

Designer:	Simon Ward
Height:	4 1/2", 11.9 cm
Colour:	White, black and red
Issued:	1995

Beswick		Price		
Number	U.S. $	Can. $	U.K. £	Aust. $
3547	—	—	39.50	—

Note: Special commission by U.K. International Ceramics Ltd. in an edition of 2,000.

3549
JERRY™

Designer:	Simon Ward
Height:	3", 7.6 cm
Colour:	Reddish brown and cream, white base
Issued:	1995

Beswick		Price		
Number	U.S. $	Can. $	U.K. £	Aust. $
3549 (Per pair with Tom)	—	—	85.00	—

Note: Special commission by U.K. International Ceramics Ltd. in an edition of 2,000.

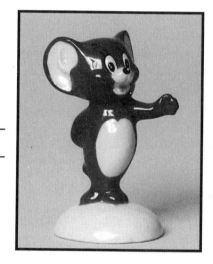

3552
TOM™

Designer:	Simon Ward
Height:	4 1/2", 11.9 cm
Colour:	Greyish blue, pink, white base
Issued:	1995

Beswick		Price		
Number	U.S. $	Can. $	U.K. £	Aust. $
3552 (Per pair with Jerry)	—	—	85.00	—

Note: Special commission by U.K. International Ceramics Ltd. in an edition of 2,000.

WALT DISNEY
CHARACTERS

1278
MICKEY MOUSE™

Designer: Jan Granoska
Height: 4", 10.1 cm
Colour: Black, white and red
Issued: 1952 - 1965

Back Stamp	Beswick Number	Price U.S. $	Can. $	U.K.£	Aust. $
Beswick Gold	1278	450.00	675.00	375.00	350.00

1279
JIMINY CRICKET™

Designer: Jan Granoska
Height: 4", 10.1 cm
Colour: Black, white, beige and blue
Issued: 1952 - 1965

Back Stamp	Beswick Number	Price U.S. $	Can. $	U.K. £	Aust. $
Beswick Gold	1279	450.00	675.00	300.00	350.00

1280
PLUTO™

Designer: Jan Granoska
Height: 3 1/2", 8.9 cm
Colour: Brown dog with red collar
Issued: 1953 - 1965

Back Stamp	Beswick Number	Price U.S. $	Can. $	U.K. £	Aust. $
Beswick Gold	1280	450.00	625.00	350.00	350.00

1281
GOOFY™

Designer:	Jan Granoska
Height:	4 1/4", 10.8 cm
Colour:	Red jersey, blue trousers, black suspenders, white gloves, brown and black hat, brown boots
Issued:	1953 - 1965

Back Stamp	Beswick Number	Price			
		U.S. $	Can. $	U.K. £	Aust. $
Beswick Gold	1281	450.00	675.00	350.00	350.00

1282
PINOCCHIO™

Designer:	Jan Granoska
Height:	4", 10.1 cm
Colour:	White and yellow jacket, red trousers, blue bowtie and shoes, brown cap
Issued:	1953 - 1965

Back Stamp	Beswick Number	Price			
		U.S. $	Can. $	U.K. £	Aust. $
Beswick Gold	1282	450.00	625.00	300.00	350.00

1283
DONALD DUCK™

Designer:	Jan Granoska
Height:	4", 10.1 cm
Colour:	White duck, blue sailor's jacket, red bow, blue and black hat
Issued:	1953 - 1965

Back Stamp	Beswick Number	Price			
		U.S. $	Can. $	U.K. £	Aust. $
Beswick Gold	1283	450.00	675.00	325.00	350.00

1289
MINNIE MOUSE™

Designer: Jan Granoska
Height: 4", 10.1 cm
Colour: Unknown
Issued: 1953 - 1965

Back Stamp	Beswick Number	Price			
		U.S. $	Can. $	U.K. £	Aust. $
Beswick Gold	1289	450.00	675.00	375.00	350.00

1291
THUMPER™

Designer: Jan Granoska
Height: 3 3/4", 9.5 cm
Colour: Grey and white rabbit, yellow, red and pink flowers on brown base
Issued: 1953 - 1965

Back Stamp	Beswick Number	Price			
		U.S. $	Can. $	U.K. £	Aust. $
Beswick Gold	1291	575.00	675.00	175.00	350.00

1301
NANA™

Designer: Jan Granoska
Height: 3 1/4", 8.3 cm
Colour: Brown dog, white frilled cap with blue ribbon
Issued: 1953 - 1965

Back Stamp	Beswick Number	Price			
		U.S. $	Can. $	U.K. £	Aust. $
Beswick Gold	1301	500.00	675.00	325.00	350.00

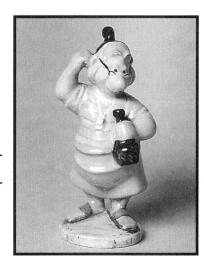

1302
SMEE™

Designer:	Jan Granoska
Height:	4 1/4", 10.8 cm
Colour:	Blue and white shirt, blue pants, red cap, green bottle
Issued:	1953 - 1965

Back Stamp	Beswick Number	U.S. $	Price Can. $	U.K. £	Aust. $
Beswick Gold	1302	450.00	700.00	175.00	350.00

1307
PETER PAN™

Designer:	Jan Granoska
Height:	5", 12.7 cm
Colour:	Light green tunic, dark green pants, brown shoes, red and green cap
Issued:	1953 - 1965

Back Stamp	Beswick Number	U.S. $	Price Can. $	U.K. £	Aust. $
Beswick Gold	1307	550.00	700.00	325.00	350.00

1312
TINKER BELL™

Designer:	Jan Granoska
Height:	5", 12.7 cm
Colour:	Light green dress, dark green wings and shoes
Issued:	1953 - 1965

Back Stamp	Beswick Number	U.S. $	Price Can. $	U.K. £	Aust. $
Beswick Gold	1312		Rare		

1325
DOPEY™

Designer:	Arthur Gredington
Height:	3 1/2", 8.9 cm
Colour:	Green coat, maroon cap, grey shoes
Issued:	1954 - 1967

Back Stamp	Beswick Number	Price U.S. $	Can. $	U.K. £	Aust. $
Beswick Gold	1325	400.00	500.00	175.00	250.00

1326
HAPPY™

Designer:	Arthur Gredington
Height:	3 1/2", 8.9 cm
Colour:	Purple tunic, light blue trousers, light brown cap, brown shoes
Issued:	1954 - 1967

Back Stamp	Beswick Number	Price U.S. $	Can. $	U.K. £	Aust. $
Beswick Gold	1326	400.00	500.00	175.00	250.00

1327
BASHFUL™

Designer:	Arthur Gredington
Height:	3 1/2", 8.9 cm
Colour:	Brown tunic, purple trousers, grey cap, brown shoes
Issued:	1954 - 1967

Back Stamp	Beswick Number	Price U.S. $	Can. $	U.K. £	Aust. $
Beswick Gold	1327	400.00	500.00	175.00	250.00

1328
SNEEZY™

Designer: Arthur Gredington
Height: 3 1/2", 8.9 cm
Colour: Green tunic, purple trousers,
brown cap and shoes
Issued: 1954 - 1967

Back Stamp	Beswick Number	U.S. $	Price Can. $	U.K. £	Aust. $
Beswick Gold	1328	400.00	500.00	175.00	250.00

1329
DOC™

Designer: Arthur Gredington
Height: 3 1/2", 8.9 cm
Colour: Brown tunic, blue trousers,
yellow cap, brown shoes
Issued: 1954 - 1967

Back Stamp	Beswick Number	U.S. $	Price Can. $	U.K. £	Aust. $
Beswick Gold	1329	400.00	500.00	200.00	250.00

1330
GRUMPY™

Designer: Arthur Gredington
Height: 3 3/4", 9.5 cm
Colour: Purple tunic, red trousers,
blue cap, brown shoes
Issued: 1954 - 1967

Back Stamp	Beswick Number	U.S. $	Price Can. $	U.K. £	Aust. $
Beswick Gold	1330	400.00	500.00	175.00	250.00

1331
SLEEPY™

Designer:	Arthur Gredington
Height:	3 1/2", 8.9 cm
Colour:	Tan tunic, red trousers, green hat, grey shoes
Issued:	1954 - 1967

Back Stamp	Beswick Number	Price U.S. $	Can. $	U.K. £	Aust. $
Beswick Gold	1331	400.00	500.00	175.00	250.00

1332A
SNOW WHITE™
Style One
First Version (Hair in Flounces)

Designer:	Arthur Gredington
Height:	5 1/2", 14.0 cm
Colour:	Yellow and purple dress, red cape, white collar
Issued:	1954 - 1955

Back Stamp	Beswick Number	Price U.S. $	Can. $	U.K. £	Aust. $
Beswick Gold	1332A		Very rare		

1332B
SNOW WHITE™
Style One
Second Version (Hair Flat to Head)

Designer:	Arthur Gredington
Height:	5 1/2", 14.0 cm
Colour:	Yellow and purple dress, red cape, white collar
Issued:	1955 - 1967

Back Stamp	Beswick Number	Price U.S. $	Can. $	U.K. £	Aust. $
Beswick Gold	1332B	750.00	875.00	400.00	500.00

2193
WINNIE THE POOH™

Designer:	Albert Hallam
Height:	2 1/2", 6.4 cm
Colour:	Golden brown and red
Issued:	1968 - 1990

Back Stamp	Beswick Number	Price U.S. $	Can. $	U.K. £	Aust. $
Beswick Gold	2193	125.00	175.00	100.00	190.00
Beswick Brown	2193	100.00	125.00	70.00	135.00

2196
EEYORE™
Style One

Designer:	Albert Hallam
Height:	2", 5.0 cm
Colour:	Grey with black markings
Issued:	1968 - 1990

Back Stamp	Beswick Number	Price U.S. $	Can. $	U.K. £	Aust. $
Beswick Gold	2196	150.00	200.00	95.00	140.00
Beswick Brown	2196	125.00	175.00	65.00	135.00

2214
PIGLET™

Designer:	Albert Hallam
Height:	2 3/4", 7.0 cm
Colour:	Pink and red
Issued:	1968 - 1990

Back Stamp	Beswick Number	Price U.S. $	Can. $	U.K. £	Aust. $
Beswick Gold	2214	150.00	200.00	95.00	165.00
Beswick Brown	2214	125.00	175.00	70.00	145.00

2215
RABBIT™

Designer: Albert Hallam
Height: 3 1/4", 8.3 cm
Colour: Brown and beige
Issued: 1968 - 1990

Back Stamp	Beswick Number	Price U.S. $	Price Can. $	Price U.K. £	Price Aust. $
Beswick Gold	2215	125.00	175.00	85.00	200.00
Beswick Brown	2215	100.00	125.00	65.00	175.00

2216
OWL™

Designer: Albert Hallam
Height: 3", 7.6 cm
Colour: Brown, white and black
Issued: 1968 - 1990

Back Stamp	Beswick Number	Price U.S. $	Price Can. $	Price U.K. £	Price Aust. $
Beswick Gold	2216	125.00	175.00	85.00	150.00
Beswick Brown	2216	100.00	150.00	60.00	135.00

2217
KANGA™
Style One

Designer: Albert Hallam
Height: 3 1/4", 8.3 cm
Colour: Dark and light brown
Issued: 1968 - 1990

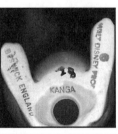

Back Stamp	Beswick Number	Price U.S. $	Price Can. $	Price U.K. £	Price Aust. $
Beswick Gold	2217	125.00	175.00	90.00	135.00
Beswick Brown	2217	100.00	150.00	60.00	135.00

2394
TIGGER™
Style One

Designer:	Graham Tongue
Height:	3", 7.6 cm
Colour:	Yellow with black stripes
Issued:	1971 - 1990

Back Stamp	Beswick Number	U.S. $	Price Can. $	U.K. £	Aust. $
Beswick Gold	2394	250.00	325.00	135.00	275.00
Beswick Brown	2394	225.00	300.00	100.00	250.00

2395
CHRISTOPHER ROBIN™
Style One

Designer:	Graham Tongue
Height:	4 3/4", 12.1 cm
Colour:	Yellow, blue and white
Issued:	1971 - 1990

Back Stamp	Beswick Number	U.S. $	Price Can. $	U.K. £	Aust. $
Beswick Gold	2395	275.00	300.00	150.00	295.00
Beswick Brown	2395	250.00	275.00	110.00	300.00

HN 3677
CINDERELLA™

Designer:	P. Parsons
Height:	8", 20.3 cm
Colour:	Blue and white dress, yellow hair
Issued:	1995 in a limited edition of 2,000
Series:	The Disney Princess Collection

Back Stamp	Doulton Number	U.S. $	Price Can. $	U.K. £	Aust. $
Doulton	HN 3677	300.00	375.00	175.00	350.00

HN 3678
SNOW WHITE™
Style Two

Designer:	P. Parsons
Height:	8 1/4", 21.0 cm
Colour:	Yellow, blue and white dress, royal blue and red cape, black hair
Issued:	1995 in a limited edition of 2,000
Series:	The Disney Princess Collection

Back Stamp	Doulton Number	Price			
		U.S. $	Can. $	U.K. £	Aust. $
Doulton	HN 3678	300.00	375.00	175.00	350.00

HN 3830
BELLE™

Designer:	P. Parsons
Height:	8", 20.3 cm
Colour:	Yellow dress and gloves, brown hair
Issued:	1996 in a limited edition of 2,000
Series:	The Disney Princess Collection

Back Stamp	Doulton Number	Price			
		U.S. $	Can. $	U.K. £	Aust. $
Doulton	HN3830	—	—	150.00	—

HN 3831
ARIEL™

Designer:	P. Parsons
Height:	8 1/4", 21.0 cm
Colour:	White dress and veil, red hair
Issued:	1996 in a limited edition of 2,000
Series:	The Disney Princess Colleciton

Back Stamp	Doulton Number	Price			
		U.S. $	Can. $	U.K. £	Aust. $
Doulton	HN 3831	—	—	150.00	—

JASMINE™

Designer:	P. Parsons
Height:	7 1/2", 19.1 cm
Colour:	Lilac dress
Issued:	1996 in a limited edition of 2,000
Series:	The Disney Princess Collection

Back Stamp		Price		
	U.S. $	Can. $	U.K. £	Aust. $
Doulton	—	—	150.00	—

Photograph not available at press time

Photograph not available at press time

SLEEPING BEAUTY™

Designer:	P. Parsons
Height:	7 1/2", 19.1 cm
Colour:	Blue dress
Issued:	1996 in a limited edition of 2,000
Series:	The Disney Princess Collection

Back Stamp		Price		
	U.S. $	Can. $	U.K. £	Aust. $
Doulton	—	—	150.00	—

WP1
WINNIE THE POOH AND THE HONEY POT™

Designer:	Unknown
Height:	2 1/2", 6.5 cm
Colour:	Yellow bear, red jersey, red-brown honey pot
Issued:	1996 to the present
Series:	Winnie the Pooh and Friends from the One Hundred Acre Wood

Back Stamp	Doulton Number		Price		
		U.S. $	Can. $	U.K. £	Aust. $
Doulton	WP1	—	—	22.50	—

Note: This set is a U.K. exclusive.

WP2
WINNIE THE POOH AND PIGLET™
The Windy Day

Designer:	Unknown
Height:	3 1/4", 8 cm
Colour:	Yellow bear, pink piglet with green suit, light brown base
Issued:	1996 to the present
Series:	Winnie the Pooh and Friends from the One Hundred Acre Wood

Back Stamp	Doulton Number	Price U.S. $	Can. $	U.K. £	Aust. $
Doulton	WP2	—	—	29.95	—

WP3
WINNIE THE POOH AND FOOTPRINTS™

Designer:	Unknown
Height:	2 3/4", 7.0 cm
Colour:	Yellow bear, red jersey
Issued:	1996 to the present
Series:	Winnie the Pooh and Friends from the One Hundred Acre Wood

Back Stamp	Doulton Number	Price U.S. $	Can. $	U.K. £	Aust. $
Doulton	WP3	—	—	19.95	—

WP4
WINNIE THE POOH IN THE ARMCHAIR™

Designer:	Unknown
Height:	3 1/4", 8 cm
Colour:	Yellow bear, pink armchair
Issued:	1996 to the present
Series:	Winnie the Pooh and Friends from the One Hundred Acre Wood

Back Stamp	Doulton Number	Price U.S. $	Can. $	U.K. £	Aust. $
Doulton	WP4	—	—	19.95	—

WP5
PIGLET AND BALLOON™

Designer: Unknown
Height: 2 3/4", 7.0 cm
Colour: Pink piglet, green suit, blue
balloon, light brown base
Issued: 1996 to the present
Series: Winnie the Pooh and Friends
from the One Hundred Acre Wood

Back Stamp	Doulton Number	Price			
		U.S. $	Can. $	U.K. £	Aust. $
Doulton	WP5	—	—	19.95	—

WP6
TIGGER™
Style Two

Designer: Unknown
Height: 1 3/4", 4.5 cm
Colour: Yellow tiger with black stripes
Issued: 1996 to the present
Series: Winnie the Pooh and Friends
from the One Hundred Acre Wood

Back Stamp	Doulton Number	Price			
		U.S. $	Can. $	U.K. £	Aust. $
Doulton	WP6	—	—	19.95	—

WP7
EEYORE™
Style Two

Designer: Unknown
Height: 3 1/4". 8 cm
Colour: Grey donkey with black markings,
pink bow
Issued: 1996 to the present
Series: Winnie the Pooh and Friends
from the One Hundred Acre Wood

Back Stamp	Doulton Number	Price			
		U.S. $	Can. $	U.K. £	Aust. $
Doulton	WP7	—	—	19.95	—

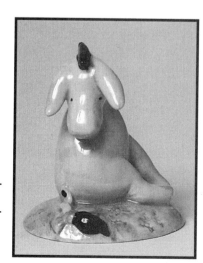

WP8
KANGA™
Style Two

Designer:	Unknown
Height:	3 1/2", 9 cm
Colour:	Dark and light brown
Issued:	1996 to the present
Series:	Winnie the Pooh and Friends from the One Hundred Acre Wood

Back Stamp	Doulton Number	Price			
		U.S. $	Can. $	U.K. £	Aust. $
Doulton	WP8	—	—	19.95	—

WP9
CHRISTOPHER ROBIN™
Style Two

Designer:	Unknown
Height:	4 1/4", 11 cm
Colour:	White and blue checkered shirt, blue shorts, black boots and reddish brown hair
Issued:	1996
Series:	Winnie the Pooh and Friends from the One Hundred Acre Wood

Back Stamp	Doulton Number	Price			
		U.S. $	Can. $	U.K. £	Aust. $
Doulton	WP9	—	—	24.95	—

WP10
CHRISTOPHER ROBIN
AND WINNIE THE POOH™

Designer:	Unknown
Height:	3 1/4", 8.5 cm
Colour:	Light blue shirt and shorts, black boots, reddish brown hair, yellow bear
Issued:	1996 to the present
Series:	Winnie the Pooh and Friends from the One Hundred Acre Wood

Back Stamp	Doulton Number	Price			
		U.S.$	Can. $	U.K. £	Aust. $
Doulton	WP10	—	—	39.95	—

WIND IN THE WILLOWS

2939
MOLE™

Designer:	Harry Sales
Modeller:	David Lyttleton
Height:	3", 7.6 cm
Colour:	Dark grey mole, brown dressing gown
Issued:	1987 - 1989

Beswick Number	Price			
	U.S. $	Can. $	U.K. £	Aust. $
2939	85.00	110.00	45.00	85.00

2940
BADGER™

Designer:	Harry Sales
Modeller:	David Lyttleton
Height:	3", 7.6 cm
Colour:	Black and white badger, salmon dressing gown
Issued:	1987 - 1989

Beswick Number	Price			
	U.S. $	Can. $	U.K. £	Aust. $
2940	85.00	110.00	45.00	85.00

2941
RATTY™

Designer:	Harry Sales
Modeller:	David Lyttleton
Height:	3 1/2", 8.9 cm
Colour:	Blue dungarees, white shirt
Issued:	1987 - 1989

Beswick Number	Price			
	U.S. $	Can. $	U.K. £	Aust. $
2941	85.00	110.00	45.00	85.00

2942
TOAD™

Designer:	Harry Sales
Modeller:	David Lyttleton
Height:	3 1/2", 8.9 cm
Colour:	Green toad, yellow waistcoat and trousers, white shirt, red bowtie
Issued:	1987 - 1989

Beswick Number		Price		
	U.S. $	Can. $	U.K. £	Aust. $
2942	85.00	110.00	45.00	85.00

3065
PORTLY™
(Otter)

Designer:	Harry Sales
Modeller:	Alan Maslankowski
Height:	2 3/4", 7.0 cm
Colour:	Brown otter, blue dungarees, green and yellow jumper, green shoes
Issued:	1988 - 1989

Beswick Number		Price		
	U.S. $	Can. $	U.K. £	Aust. $
3065	200.00	225.00	120.00	135.00

3076
WEASEL GAMEKEEPER™

Designer:	Harry Sales
Modeller:	Alan Maslankowski
Height:	4", 10.1 cm
Colour:	Brown weasel, green jacket, trousers and cap, yellow waistcoat
Issued:	1988 - 1989

Beswick Number		Price		
	U.S. $	Can. $	U.K. £	Aust. $
3076	200.00	225.00	120.00	135.00

INDICES

ALPHABETICAL INDEX

NUMERICAL INDEX

BEATRIX POTTER STUDIO SCULPTURES

BEDTIME CHORUS

BESWICK BEARS

ROYAL DOULTON BRAMBLEY HEDGE

ROYAL DOULTON BUNNYKINS

BESWICK COUNTRY COUSINS

254

257

M ARNALEA A NTIQUES

THE DOULTON SPECIALIST
SERVING COLLECTORS SINCE 1974!

We carry
One of Canada's Largest Collections of
DISCONTINUED ROYAL DOULTON

FIGURINES • JUGS • ANIMALS • PLATES
SERIESWARE • LAMBETH • ROYAL WORCESTER

MAILING LIST AVAILABLE

Our Selection's Great - Our Prices Competitive -
and the GST is Always Included!

51 MAIN STREET NORTH,
CAMPBELLVILLE ONTARIO L0P 1B0
905-854-0287

PRECIOUS MEMORIES MUSEUM & OUTLET
-Eastern Canada's Largest Doulton Dealer-

FIGURINES	TABLEWARE	JUGS
BRAMBLY HEDGE	BESWICK	BEATRIX POTTER
BUNNYKINS	SNOWMEN	ANIMALS

FANTASTIC PRICES: ASK FOR OUR PRICE LIST
WE BUY • WE SELL • WE SHIP ORDERS
WANTED ---- ALL DOULTON ITEMS
TOP PRICES PAID

George & Nora Bagnall — **PRECIOUS MEMORIES**
Phone: (902) 368-1212 — *89 Trans Canada Hwy.*
Fax: (902) 368-7321 — *Charlottetown, P.E.I*
Orders: 1-800-463-5200 — *Canada, C1E 1E8*

WILLIAM CROSS
ANTIQUES & COLLECTABLES INC.

DOULTON-BESWICK STORYBOOK FIGURES

BEATRIX POTTER
BIRDS, ANIMALS
WHIMSIES
TABLEWARE
DECORATIVE WARE

Call or Send for Current List:
4631 East Hastings
Burnaby, B.C. V5C 2K6
Tel: (604) 298-9599
Fax: (604) 298-9563
Outside B.C.: 1-800-639-7771

We Buy — **We Sell**

YOURS & MINE LTD.

- **FIGURINES**
- **TOBIES**
- **PLATES**
- **BELLS**

ROYAL DOULTON, BUNNYKINS BEATRIX POTTER, HUMMEL FIGURINES, ETC.

Box No. 22055
Westmount Post Office
Waterloo, Ontario — (519) 744-8059
Canada N2L 6J7 — (519) 836-6757

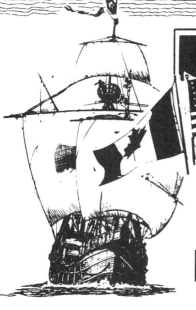

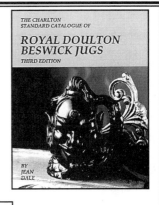

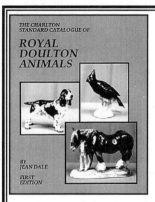

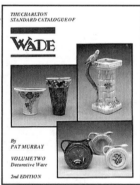